SHADOW
GOVERNMENT

SHADOW
GOVERNMENT

How the Secret Global Elite
Is Using Surveillance Against You

GRANT R. JEFFREY

BEST-SELLING AUTHOR OF *THE NEXT WORLD WAR*

WATERBROOK
PRESS

SHADOW GOVERNMENT
PUBLISHED BY WATERBROOK PRESS
12265 Oracle Boulevard, Suite 200
Colorado Springs, Colorado 80921

ISBN 978-1-4000-7442-6
ISBN 978-0-307-45831-5 (electronic book)

Published in the United States by WaterBrook Multnomah, an imprint of the Crown Publishing Group, a division of Random House Inc., New York.

Library of Congress Cataloging-in-Publication Data
Jeffrey, Grant R.
  Shadow government : how the secret global elite is using surveillance against you / Grant R. Jeffrey. — 1st ed.
      p. cm.
  Includes bibliographical references.
  ISBN 978-1-4000-7442-6 — ISBN 978-0-307-45831-5 (electronic)
  1. Leadership. 2. Electronic surveillance. 3. Elite (Social sciences) 4. Globalization. I. Title.
  HM1263.J44 2009
  236'.9—dc22

                              2009020536

Printed in the United States of America
2009—First Edition

10 9 8 7 6 5 4 3 2 1

SPECIAL SALES
Most WaterBrook Multnomah books are available at special quantity discounts when purchased in bulk by corporations, organizations, and special-interest groups. Custom imprinting or excerpting can also be done to fit special needs. For information, please e-mail SpecialMarkets@WaterBrookMultnomah.com or call 1-800-603-7051.

CONTENTS

ACKNOWLEDGMENTS

Shadow Government is an exploration of the growing threats to our privacy and freedom from the relentless development of surveillance technologies and the willingness of governments to exercise those technologies against their own citizens—as well as foreign nationals. This book explores how globalist strategies and the phenomenal growth and expansion of surveillance capabilities are setting the stage for the rise of the Antichrist—the global dictator prophesied in the Bible. The Antichrist will arise in our generation.

We are part of the first generation in human history that can identify the trends and understand how current political and technological developments will make it possible for a future dictator to achieve the totalitarian control of the world's population. Technology will be a primary tool used to implement the system of the Mark of the Beast.

This book is the result of more than forty years of research involving the study of thousands of books and articles, augmented by interviews with political leaders and experts in intelligence, military strategy, and surveillance technologies, as well as the intensive study of the Scriptures. As this book will demonstrate, the trends we see unfolding in our day represent the greatest threats ever presented to the freedom and privacy of humanity. However, our faith and hope for the future are grounded upon the promise of our Lord Jesus Christ: "And when these things begin to come to pass, then look up, and lift up your heads; for your redemption draweth nigh" (Luke 21:28).

My loving parents have inspired in me a profound love for Jesus Christ and the prophetic truths that are revealed in the Word of God. When I was a teenager, my father took me to prophecy conferences that often led us to discuss world events in light of Bible prophecy.

I dedicate this book to my wife, Kaye. She is a continuing inspiration to my work and a faithful partner in our ministry. I trust that the information revealed in the following pages will encourage you to study the Bible's prophecies about the last days and the triumphant return of Jesus Christ to set up His Kingdom on earth.

Dr. Grant R. Jeffrey
Toronto, Ontario
July 2009

THE HIDDEN FACE OF THE SHADOW GOVERNMENT

In Western democracies, citizens are accustomed to voting for their represent-atives in government. Democratic principles and national constitutions assure us of a voice in determining the policies and powers that rule us. What most of us don't realize, however, is that these rules have changed profoundly. These changes endanger us in a multitude of ways, but no one gave us a chance to vote on the political transformation.

We have already entered the era of the *shadow government,* a term I will use in this book to refer to powerful agencies that collect data on every one of us. The shadow government observes our private lives and monitors our finances. It tracks your movements and mine. It listens in on our communications, records our purchases, and archives our decisions and preferences in permanent computer files.

The natural reaction to hearing this is to say, "They have no right to do that!" In a truly democratic society, the power lies with the people and not with the government. But in this era of the shadow government, we have lost most of our personal rights. And the loss of our privacy is one of the most evident and most ominous outcomes.

You have no say in determining what they learn about you and how they use the information. Because this unelected authority operates in the shadows, it is not subject to meaningful oversight by any democratic institution or recognized arm of government. Intelligence agencies, legislative bodies, the courts, regulatory agencies—no center of elected, democratic political power has any real authority over the shadow government.

We are living in a dangerous time, when governments throughout the world have allowed an unprecedented network of shadow governments to grow and consolidate power. Those who are starting to control our lives from the shadows conduct massive surveillance and exert extensive military power in countries around the world. While these activities are largely invisible to ordinary citizens, elected governments are aware of the shift in power.

THE UPHEAVAL FOLLOWING 9/11

When radical Muslims hijacked four commercial airliners on September 11, 2001, and commandeered them on suicide missions to attack the World Trade Center and the Pentagon, we all realized the world had changed in a way that was hard to accept. What we didn't see coming was the way this attack on American soil would introduce a profound shift in power in Western nations. In response to the now-visible threat of Islamist movements against democratic countries, governments took drastic action, making unprecedented changes in national security measures. This went far beyond tighter security at airports and military action in Afghanistan and Iraq. Ostensibly to protect the free citizens of their nations, governments intensified their surveillance of *all* of us.

A troubling feature of modern society is that the security measures taken by governments have become increasingly secretive. Governments can spy on anyone without due cause or due process. They no longer have to obtain judicial approval, undergo legislative review, or be held accountable to any elected body, such as a senate or parliamentary subcommittee. The real political power is now hidden so that no one but insiders and intelligence agencies knows who wields power at the top levels of national governments. Increasingly, anonymous military, intelligence, and security officials have taken control of Western societies in the name of national security.

If you wonder how this could happen, consider two things. First, there is the constant threat of attack from rogue nations, radical Muslim terrorists, and antidemocratic forces in possession of weapons of mass destruction. And second, there are the rapid and extensive advancements in invasive technology, a critical tool in the hands of those who make the calls for the shadow government. These two developments have converged to shift the power away from elected governments and into the hands of hidden decision makers.

All of this has prophetic significance, which we will explore in a later chapter. It is no accident that the necessary technology exists to enable a world dictator, for the first time in history, to control the earth's population. As intellectual and political elites take over the levers of power, consolidating their control over scientific, economic, and military technologies, the shadow government can secretly manipulate the entire world. And not just the world as a whole, but the lives of individual citizens. No one is protected from their invasive surveillance.

The religious intellectual Pierre Teilhard de Chardin pointed out the overwhelming power that would be wielded by a group of brilliant thinkers dedicated to the cause of unrivaled world government. He wrote, "Nothing in the universe can resist the cumulative ardor of a sufficiently large number of enlightened minds working together in organized groups."[1]

Almost a century ago, John Buchan, an important figure in post–World War I British politics, wrote an intriguing novel titled *The Power-House.* In it he explored a fictional group of extremely wealthy and powerful individuals who moved behind the scenes of politics, international finance, and business to subvert the national sovereignty of Western governments. The goal of this group was to create and control a system of global government. A self-appointed group of wealthy individuals allied with Western politicians and former key political leaders would hold the *real* power over democratic nations.[2]

HOW THE RULERS WENT INTO HIDING

Until the last century, political power was concentrated in very public and widely venerated leaders such as kings, governors, and even dictators who were not shy about making known their power to rule their nations. Some went out of their way to remind citizens exactly who was in control, such as the public displays and massive monuments used by Adolf Hitler in Germany and Joseph Stalin in the Soviet Union.

However, in the last half of the twentieth century and the beginning of the twenty-first, a new political power paradigm came into being. In place of highly visible leaders, we now have elected representatives who exert only limited control, while the real power resides with a separate group. The most powerful individuals who control our nations and our lives do their work behind the scenes. They are joined by current and retired political leaders who, along with certain wealthy and influential figures, form an open conspiracy to produce a new global government. Their goal is to replace all existing independent democratic governments.

This is the sort of thing we tend to associate with nations that do not have a long history of democracy. However, the hidden leaders of shadow governments operate in both totalitarian and democratic governments throughout the world. Since the end of World War II, the secret globalist elites have been bolstered by political, financial, military, and governmental leaders from North America and Western Europe.

Just as our generation was transformed by the attacks of 9/11, the world was changed almost a century earlier by the terrible devastation of World War I. For the first time, Western nations saw that a massive war could annihilate humanity. The First World War introduced chemical weapons, poison gas, machine guns, and artillery that killed more than forty million soldiers and civilians. (I include in these figures casualties of the 1918–22 Russian civil war.)

Many of the leaders of Western nations concluded that the most pressing global need was to eliminate the possibility of a future genocidal world war. That concern gave birth to the formulation of a New World Order, which in theory would eliminate the possibility of a future world war. The stated goal of this globalist agenda was to protect humanity from the devastating technology of war. To protect us from another world war, they reasoned, it would be necessary to eliminate every one of the sovereign, independent nations that could wage war against any other state.

In the protracted negotiations of the Paris Peace Conference of 1919, a number of key Western leaders came to believe that the only way to preserve humanity was to form a partnership involving the real, secret leadership of numerous Western nations. In the name of protecting the world's population from future war, this secret group subverted the historic system of sovereign governments.

Initially, they created the League of Nations, which proved to be ineffective. Despite good intentions, the League of Nations failed to prevent the outbreak of a second world war. German, Italian, and Japanese aggression bathed the world in the blood of more than sixty million dead before the Allied victory in 1945.

During and following World War II, those who had hoped but failed to create a global government renewed their efforts. In light of possible unrestricted nuclear war between the Soviet Union and the United States (and later, China), they formulated a new international body that came to be known as the United Nations (UN). What wasn't announced publicly is that the UN was the global elitists' next step in launching in embryonic form the coming world government.

Members of the Council on Foreign Relations (created after WWI and still a powerful influence toward global government) virtually wrote the UN charter. This group was dedicated to the proposition that the sovereign states of the West must be secretly joined in a global compact that would make future war impossible. While the goal of world peace was laudable, the unfortunate result was that the foundation for a global government was laid without the knowledge of or approval from the citizens of the Western nations that were affected.

THE COMING EVIL

It will be difficult for many readers to accept my argument that widely respected political and business leaders would support plans to eliminate the United States and its Constitution in favor of the tyranny of a secret global elite. However, as we will see in later chapters, a series of international crises changed the thinking of these leaders, spurring the consolidation of power in the shadow government. Two world wars, the proliferation of nuclear weapons and other weapons of mass destruction, and the constant threat of attack from radical Muslim forces fuel the move toward globalism. And what we have seen so far is only a hint of what is to come.

We are rapidly approaching the greatest crisis in history. Jesus Christ warned that humanity would experience an unprecedented crisis just before He returned to establish His eternal Kingdom on earth. Jesus prophesied a "great tribulation, such as was not since the beginning of the world to this time, no, nor ever shall be" (Matthew 24:21). The prophet Daniel foretold that the terrible time of tribulation will last seven years and will conclude with the battle of Armageddon and the Messiah's triumphant return to earth (see Daniel 9:24–27). The biblical prophets also warned that the most evil man in history would arise during the final generation of this age. This man will be empowered by Satan to seize political, economic, military, and religious control first in Europe (as the revived Roman Empire) and then over the entire world population. This mysterious individual is identified by several names throughout Scripture, including the "lawless one" (2 Thessalonians 2:8–9, NIV), the "man of sin" (2 Thessalonians 2:3), "that Wicked" (2 Thessalonians 2:8; 1 John 3:12; 5:18), and even "the mystery of iniquity" (2 Thessalonians 2:7). Yet most people know him by the name used by the prophet John, who called him the "antichrist" (see 2 John 7). This completely evil man will embody Satan's ages-long passion to set himself up as god to be worshiped by all of humanity.

You and I will live to see the most terrifying dictator in history arise to rule the world. He will embody pure evil, and he will demand that all people worship him as their only god or they will be annihilated.

TECHNOLOGY IN THE HANDS OF THE ANTICHRIST

In the past it was difficult to understand how any individual could exert complete control over humanity, as is foretold in the Bible. The book of Revelation, for example, describes devastating military attacks from the air, the deliberate poisoning of one-third of the planet's land and water, and the destruction of two-thirds of the earth's population. Serious students of the Bible naturally wondered how these predictions could be fulfilled. Did the prophecies speak of actual future events, or were they only allegorical symbols referring to a spiritual war between the forces of good and evil? In our generation we know enough about warfare, technology, and shifting political allegiances that we can begin to see how one man could exercise such power throughout the world. For the first time in history, it is possible to contemplate the potential for humanity's complete destruction in a global war.

In the chapters that follow, we will look at prophecies that describe the Antichrist's rise to power and the nature of the global government that he will control. The Antichrist will become the dominant political, military, and religious figure in the world. God revealed these truths to awaken Christians to the signs of Christ's return to earth, when He will take His followers home to heaven.

The rise of the shadow government has significant prophetic implications. The rush to global government, paired with astonishing developments in surveillance technology, will enable the totalitarian regime of the Antichrist to introduce his dreaded Mark of the Beast system. If you know what to look for, you will see all around you measures that could make this system of global control transform into true world government.

America's national sovereignty has been progressively eroded. One obvious example, seen almost daily in the news, is the fallout from the threat of global warming. To address this environmental issue, various UN treaties demand that American laws be harmonized with those of other nations in the name of globalization. The issue is much larger than responding to global warming. With the loss of national sovereignty, we will also lose rights and freedoms we now take for granted. Over time, we will no longer enjoy the benefits of free enterprise, and we will lose the guarantees of political, economic, and religious freedom. The leaders that operate behind the scenes have adopted a philosophy of globalism, sharing the desire to become global citizens of the New World Order.

YOU ARE BEING WATCHED

You don't have to look far to see early indications of our loss of freedom. Following the terrorist attacks on the World Trade Center and the Pentagon in 2001, national governments around the world broadened and accelerated spying activities against their own citizens. The creation of a total surveillance society has set the stage for the totalitarian police state described two thousand years ago by the prophet John in the book of Revelation. In later chapters, we will examine the growing use of radio frequency identification (RFID) technology, which is only one step removed from implanting computer chips beneath the skin of every person. This technology could easily be laying the groundwork for the fulfillment of John's prophecy about the totalitarian police state that will rule the world during the last three and a half years of this age, before Christ returns at Armageddon. The development of computerized information warfare can neutralize an enemy's economy, defenses, and infrastructure. Weapons using powerful electromagnetic forces can influence a country's weather, destroy a nation's computer systems, and even influence the mental processes of individuals. These technological advances give us a more detailed idea of the prophesied Mark of the Beast system and show how the Antichrist would be able to establish unrivaled global domination (see Revelation 13:16–18).

In later chapters we will look more closely at these developments, and we will examine the shifting geopolitical alliances between America, Europe, Russia, China, the Arab states, and Israel. A massive shift in the balance of power is laying the groundwork for the unprecedented military battles to come in the last days.

GOD'S DESCRIPTION OF THE LAST DAYS

A number of prophecies teach that Jesus Christ will return from heaven to take all true Christians home to the New Jerusalem in heaven. This will take place immediately prior to the seven-year Tribulation period, which will begin when the Antichrist signs a seven-year treaty with Israel. Christ's promise to Christians is the "blessed hope" (Titus 2:13), which also is known as the Rapture. We are commanded by the Lord to rejoice in our continuing expectation that "when Christ, who is our life, shall appear, then shall ye also appear with him in glory" (Colossians 3:4). The message of prophecy is not one of doom and gloom, as some critics have suggested. Rather, Jesus commanded His followers to respond with joyful anticipation when they begin to see the fulfillment of these prophecies.

Some Christians who are critical of prophecy teachers, including me, accuse us of being sensationalists because we take the prophecies so seriously. We are led to determine whether these predictions are being fulfilled by events occurring in our generation. The best evidence clearly indicates that we are living in the last days.

This is far from sensationalism. The Word of God commands believers to carefully consider the prophetic passages of the Scriptures. The apostle Peter assures us that "we have also a more sure word of prophecy; whereunto ye do well that ye take heed, as unto a light that shineth in a dark place, until the day dawn, and the day star arise in your hearts" (2 Peter 1:19). Of the more than thirty-one thousand verses found in the Bible, more than one in four (27 percent) focus on prophecy. This suggests the tremendous importance of God's prophetic message.

The great scientist Sir Isaac Newton was fascinated with Bible prophecy. The discovery of thousands of his unpublished manuscripts in an attic at Cambridge University revealed that he wrote many more research notes and manuscripts about prophecy than he did on scientific matters. In his book *Observations upon the Prophecies of Daniel, and the Apocalypse of St. John,* Newton wrote, "And the giving ear to the Prophets is a fundamental character of the true Church. For God has so ordered the Prophecies, that in the latter days 'the wise may understand, but the wicked shall do wickedly, and none of the wicked shall understand' (Daniel 12:9–10)."[3]

I agree completely with Newton's conclusion. As we will discover in this book, the evidence points to the fulfillment of God's plan in this generation. We will witness the sobering and yet faith-building events that were prophesied more than two thousand years ago.

At the center of Satan's attempt to use the Antichrist to take over the world—before his ultimate defeat at the hands of the Messiah—are the work, strategies, and agenda of the shadow government. At the top of that agenda is the destruction of your privacy.

PART I

TECHNOLOGY THAT DESTROYS YOUR PRIVACY

CHAPTER 1

YOU HAVE NO MORE PRIVACY

In the War Against Privacy, You Are the Target

An undeclared but very real war is being waged on your privacy and freedom. Your movements, personal communications, preferences, loyalties, habits—all these things are no longer private. And in spite of the fact that our privacy and liberty are under attack on multiple fronts, the average citizen in the Western world seems blissfully unaware of the threat.

We assume that our privacy, "the right to be left alone," is secure. We couldn't be more wrong. High-tech surveillance methods used by governments responding to the threats of terrorism, drug trafficking, tax evasion, and organized crime are stealing one of your most basic human rights—the right to privacy, the right to be left alone.

THE ALL-SEEING EYES

An interesting metaphor for the invasive surveillance society is found in a fascinating proposal for eighteenth-century prison reform. In 1785 philosopher and legal reformer Jeremy Bentham advocated that the English government build a state-of-the-art prison to more efficiently observe and guard dangerous prisoners with twenty-four-hour surveillance. Bentham's proposed Panopticon prison called for the use of optical instruments and mirrors to allow a very small team of guards stationed in a central tower to observe hundreds of prisoners. Bentham's system was designed in such a way that prisoners would never know when they were under active surveillance.

The idea was that the fear of continuous surveillance would motivate inmates to police their own behavior. Tragically, the practical application of Bentham's nightmare vision is becoming reality in the twenty-first century. Advanced surveillance technologies available to government, corporations, and even your neighbors have created a twenty-four-hour, 365-day, total-surveillance society—the same system that would have violated the privacy of British prison inmates in 1785.

The current British home secretary, Jacqui Smith, exercises political control over all UK counterintelligence operations. This includes Scotland Yard's Counter Terrorism Command, the Security Service (MI5), and Government Communications Headquarters (GCHQ), the British government's global eavesdropping operation. Smith is working to establish an enormous computer database that would collect for analysis every telephone call, all Internet searches, and all e-mails being transmitted within or outside of the United Kingdom.[1]

Your Life on Camera

Smith's plans are but one manifestation of the all-seeing, all-hearing surveillance. The installation of closed-circuit television (CCTV) cameras in public places makes our daily activities, including our private interactions, a matter for close examination by unseen observers. My wife, Kaye, and I conducted a research trip in the United Kingdom in 2008. Although I had previously documented the massive adoption of CCTV by local councils and national authorities in the UK, I was stunned to see the extraordinary expansion of that type of surveillance. By the end of 2008, millions of CCTV cameras were monitoring the activities of every citizen and visitor in the country. The United Kingdom, the mother of Western political freedom and democracy, is now the most obsessively watched society in the West.

Surveillance cameras followed us during every step of our passage through

UK customs and British immigration at Heathrow Airport. And it didn't stop there. We were on camera as we acquired a car at the rental car agency office and as we proceeded out of the airport parking garage. As we entered the main highway, we noticed traffic-control cameras monitoring virtually every mile and covering every road, even in small towns. More than two thousand car-recognition cameras capture photos of cars, license plates, and drivers along with their passengers. Cameras recorded us as we purchased gas and food. Recent estimates by British authorities suggest that citizens and tourists alike will be captured on camera an average of five hundred times every day. Even London's city buses are outfitted with an astonishing sixty thousand cameras, in addition to the ten thousand CCTV cameras on subway cars and trains.

But despite the almost universal presence of CCTV, even in back alleys, law enforcement authorities report that the cameras have not suppressed violent crime as much as they have displaced it. Surveillance cameras motivate criminals to move their activities a few blocks away—to a location with less-active CCTV surveillance.

A few years ago a million CCTV systems were operating in the United Kingdom. However, a 2008 article in the *Guardian* stated that an astounding *4.2 million* CCTV cameras were being used in the surveillance of UK citizens and tourists.[2]

Cameras That Hear

It now goes far beyond simple cameras mounted on utility poles. Scientists have developed "listening" cameras that, paired with artificial intelligence software, recognize particular sounds such as gunshots, car crashes, and breaking glass. In response to certain sounds, the camera rotates and captures what could be a criminal or terrorist act. Despite the enormous financial cost and the invasiveness of the CCTV system, a report by the UK Home Office concluded that better street lighting is seven times more effective in preventing crime.

If watching you and listening to what you are saying is not enough, some new versions of CCTV technology enable police supervisors to confront you verbally through a speaker system. Law enforcement personnel can issue an immediate warning if they feel you are engaging in illegal behavior. And just in case all of this has not been disturbing enough for you, some UK municipalities are *broadcasting* local CCTV coverage on television. They ask citizens to tune in and watch so they can inform on the activities of their neighbors. Welcome to the world of block informers, a system you thought was limited to the horrors committed by the Nazis, the Soviets, and Communist China.

CCTV surveillance doesn't end with cameras posted in public places. Miniature security cameras designed to promote safety and control crime on private property are now used for vastly expanded purposes. Companies use CCTV for the continual surveillance of employees during work-hours. They are observed at their desks, in washrooms, and throughout the office area. Employers justify the spying operations against employees, vendors, clients, customers, and visitors as a way to combat theft and industrial espionage. No matter what reasons are used to justify the surveillance, you are losing your privacy in just about every setting imaginable.

We live in a total surveillance environment that closely resembles the horror described by George Orwell in his famous novel *1984*. Orwell described a future global regime composed of three totalitarian governments. In comparison to his horrific vision, computer technologies developed in the last few decades have created a daily environment far more threatening than any faced by the character Winston in *1984*.

THEY KNOW EVERYTHING ABOUT YOU

The loss of privacy goes far beyond having your public activities monitored on camera. Scott McNealy, CEO of Sun Microsystems, declared some time ago that "privacy is dead, deal with it."[3]

There are legal means that individuals and businesses can use to acquire and store information about you, obtained from your use of the Internet and even from such ordinary activities as shopping for groceries, buying a movie ticket, or ordering items online. You might think that you don't provide information to governments, law enforcement agencies, and marketers. However, you are dispensing vast amounts of personal information every time you use a check, credit card, or debit card. Every time you make a purchase using these forms of payment, you supply information on your bank account, financial history, buying habits, and product preferences.

It seems that no information about you is insignificant. Your Internet searches, your online shopping, the e-mails you send, and the Web sites you access—all of these are of interest to someone. The subjects that attract you, the causes you support, your brand preferences, the topics you research on the Web, your reading habits online—all of these are important to Web site operators. Everything you do on the Internet, including visiting Web sites and chat rooms, sending and receiving e-mail, researching health issues and medical questions, and shopping is permanently recorded in a computer database. Google, the most popular Internet search engine, has admitted that it gathers and stores information on every one of the more than 330 million Internet searches completed every day.

What's more, every e-mail you've ever sent or received and all the online searches you have completed are available to police and intelligence agencies. Who is so careful in what they say in private e-mails that they would never include a statement that might someday be considered suspicious to certain government authorities? And who considers the potential damage to their future career plans or credit rating that could result from research they have done using the Internet? For example, an innocent medical search to gain information about a disease such as Alzheimer's, even if you are doing the research for a relative or friend, could be accessed by an investigator during a background check when you apply for a job. Even the possibility of a link between a prospective employee and a devastating disease could be sufficient cause to reject your employment application.[4]

Your Entire History on Exhibit

Attacks on privacy are not new. Beginning in 1917, after destroying the first elected government of Russia, the new communist dictatorship of Lenin began a process of secret police surveillance of its entire society. Even in the democratic nations of the West, government intelligence and police agencies created a surveillance system to monitor citizens' activities. Prior to this war on privacy, only the few individuals suspected of criminal activity, sabotage, or sedition were considered worthy of police surveillance. But now, with rapid advances in sophisticated surveillance devices and computer technologies, most national governments have developed an intense interest in every citizen. Governments gather enormous amounts of previously private information on the assets, activities, communications, financial transactions, health, and political and religious activities of virtually every person on earth—and with relative ease.

Many military intelligence agencies, government agencies, and large corporations have introduced sophisticated security systems requiring employees to wear a badge containing a radio frequency identification microchip. This RFID chip enables companies, agencies, and organizations to monitor the location and activity of every worker during every moment he or she is on the premises. When an employee enters the office, a computer records the exact time and begins monitoring his or her every move throughout the day. Security sensors at strategic locations throughout the office complex record the location and duration of the activities of the badge wearer.

Many office phone systems monitor all private phone calls made by employees while at work. Computerized phone systems maintain a permanent record of all known phone numbers of clients, customers, and vendors. If an employee places a personal call, the phone system records the unauthorized number and produces a report of the employee's private calls, along with the duration of such calls. This data can be used against the employee at the next performance evaluation.[5]

It's interesting that U.S. corporations are using secret employee surveillance more than businesses in any other nation. The American Civil Liberties Union has warned, "Criminals have more privacy rights than employees. Police have to get a court order [to eavesdrop on suspected criminals], whereas in the workplace, surveillance can be conducted without safeguards."[6] Computer network security supervisors in many companies go as far as to monitor the keystrokes and productivity of all employees who use a computer in their work. Employees often complain about the stress they experience knowing they are being monitored constantly throughout the day. In many companies, computer spyware monitors an employee's Internet activities. Add to this the growing use of random drug testing, secret cameras in washrooms, and intrusive psychological questionnaires. The bottom line is that companies are creating an adversarial and unhealthy psychological environment for workers.

You should be appalled to know that your local and state police, federal intelligence agencies, government officials, employers, and even curious neighbors and business competitors can acquire virtually all of your private information. A record of your travel destinations, the newspapers and books you read, your video rentals, your pay-TV choices, your traffic tickets, your medical tests, as well as your private purchases are recorded in computer files. Anyone with enough computer knowledge can access your information, legally or not.

There is a growing public awareness and concern about the numerous attacks on our privacy through the misuse of computer records. However, the United States Congress and Canada's Parliament have failed to enact serious laws to protect the privacy of citizens' medical, criminal, and financial records.

Your Secret Life Now on Camera

Security companies that work under contract for large corporations have found ways to make use of advances in surveillance devices. Virtually invisible pinhole cameras can be placed behind a wall to monitor everything that goes on in an adjacent room, both visually and audibly. The tiny lens, which is the size of a pinhead, is unnoticeable. Infrared cameras can record images silently and in near-total darkness. Another type of surveillance camera can be concealed in a mobile telephone, recording events through the tiny hole normally used for the microphone. This tool often is used for industrial espionage, stealing trade secrets from a competitor. It is also useful in gaining the upper hand in business negotiations. For example, during a face-to-face meeting in a protracted negotiation, the user of the cell phone can leave the phone in the boardroom when he exits to take a break. As the other team discusses their strategy, supposedly in private, the cell phone is recording the conversation.

Surveillance devices are also being used much more widely by individuals. For several hundred dollars, you can obtain a device that enables you to monitor every conversation that takes place in your home or office while you are away. A remote monitoring device known as the XPS-1000 allows you to listen to conversations in your office or home by using the telephone. From a remote location, you dial your phone number using a secret activation code. The phone will not ring, but from that moment on, you can monitor every sound in the room where the phone is located. Another tiny device, a microtransmitter powered for three months by a miniature battery, can be left in any room and will broadcast for a distance of up to one thousand yards to a hidden radio receiver–tape recorder.

While fascinating, the miniaturization of cameras, microphones, and recording devices has stolen what was left of our privacy. If a person is determined to monitor your activities, you can't prevent it. You can try to guard your privacy by using a software program or device designed to protect your communications. But in doing so, you will have inadvertently alerted intelligence agencies and private investigators that you have something worth keeping private. This may cause them to increase the level of surveillance in an attempt to discover why you want to avoid it.

Abuse of Legitimate Data

All U.S. intelligence agencies, including the Bureau of Alcohol, Tobacco, Firearms, and Explosives (ATF) and the Federal Bureau of Investigation (FBI), can access data from the National Identification Center to identify and monitor every registered gun owner in the United States. However, we have to ask this question: what else will government agencies pursue using legitimate and legally acquired data?

Two of America's most secretive agencies, the National Reconnaissance Office (NRO) and the National Security Agency (NSA), maintain a massive global surveillance system known as Project Echelon. This system can monitor every telephone call, fax, Internet search, and e-mail transmission worldwide. (We will look more closely at the remarkable capabilities of this massive surveillance system in chapter 5.) We need to face the sobering truth that we can't escape the growing surveillance capabilities of all governments, both East and West. These developments turn our attention to the last-days prophecy from the book of Revelation about a coming totalitarian police system. John warned that a person's every activity will be controlled: "That no man might buy or sell, save he that had the mark, or the name of the beast, or the number of his name" (Revelation 13:17). Remarkably, John was describing a universal population-control system that would impose some kind of numerical identification on every person in order to monitor his or her financial transactions, trade, business, and ability to buy and sell. This system will enable law enforcement authorities working for the Antichrist and his partner, the False Prophet (see Revelation 13:16), to control the world's population through a unique ID, based on the number 666, on everyone's right hand or forehead. The recent subcutaneous pet identification chips could easily be inserted in each human being.

WHO WANTS TO CONTROL YOU?

Government authorities, national security agencies, and businesses that market and sell consumer products know far more about you than most of your friends and family will ever know. People you will never meet have compiled personal information about the details of your daily life, place of residence, type of residence, spending habits, and financial assets. Government agencies justify the invasion of your privacy by reminding us of the threats posed by international terrorism, organized crime, the influx of illegal immigrants, and citizens who defraud the government as welfare cheats or tax evaders.

The NSA possesses detailed records of millions of U.S. citizens, including your communications, health status, medical treatments, employment status, vehicle ownership, driving record, criminal record, and real-estate holdings. In addition, all of your credit records, banking and financial transactions, credit rating, educational transcripts, and travel records are available to many major corporations and government research institutes.

Your life is also of great interest to foreign governments. Most of the Western democratic governments, as well as the governments of China and Russia, are thought to maintain enormous computer databases filled with details about millions of U.S. citizens. Data storage is just the first step. Next will be the most effective ways to organize, categorize, and use this private information. This hurdle will be removed when the government assigns a unique identification number to each citizen. Once that is accomplished, the staggering number of separate files on individual citizens in various databases can be combined into a single massive intelligence file. (We will talk more about this process in chapter 3.)

A confirmation of the consolidation of citizen data was publicized in the Canadian press on May 19, 2000. The Canadian government reluctantly confirmed that up to two thousand significant pieces of information had been assembled on virtually every Canadian citizen in a massive database known as the Longitudinal Labor Force File. As a result of strident public criticism following these revelations, the Canadian government promised to destroy the computer program that linked these files. However, the federal government admitted they still will retain computer data on more than thirty million Canadians—data that are retained in separate computer files held by a variety of government departments, including the Canadian Security Intelligence Service (CSIS), Royal Canadian Mounted Police (RCMP), Immigration, and provincial police forces.[7]

A SECRET CHIP IN YOUR CREDIT CARDS

Your credit and debit cards are much more than a convenient way to pay for goods and services. The magnetic strip on a credit card or debit card holds electronic data verifying your identity, as well as information validating your right to access particular computer databases, such as your bank accounts. More and more, these cards are being replaced by higher-security smart cards that contain even more information about you. A smart card contains an embedded RFID chip capable of holding millions of times more digital information than is contained in a card's magnetic strip.

Smart cards provide high levels of security, since they are capable of storing

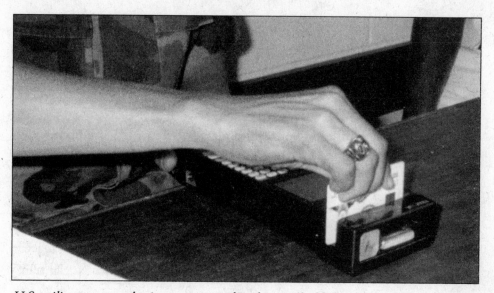

U.S. military personnel using a smart card with an embedded radio frequency identification chip.

biometric information, such as the iris pattern in the eye of the authorized user. These new cards will document the user's identity by measuring 173 distinct characteristics from the rings, burrows, and filaments within the iris. The stored data is compared with an iris scan made by a surveillance camera that can read your iris pattern from a distance of several yards.

Other identifying data include your precise hand geometry, which involves identifying you by measuring the length of your fingers and the translucence and thickness of your skin. Infrared scanners can reveal and record the patterns of veins on your palm or the back of your hand. Voice-recognition software can confirm your identity through digital measurement of your voice tone and timbre. Incredibly, a new machine can puff air over the back of your hand, analyze your subtle body odors, and detect as many as thirty separate trace chemical elements that supply a positive identification reading.[8] All of this data, and more, can be stored in an RFID chip.

Soon you will be able to replace your credit and debit cards with one very secure smart card that is virtually immune to counterfeiting and attacks by hackers. The data will be encrypted, and your unique passwords—including biometric information—will be required for you to use the card. More than two and a half billion radio frequency smart cards now in use worldwide can perform these functions:

- cash transactions such as rechargeable stored-value cards that carry a predetermined monetary value
- confidential transferring of medical data to paramedics and hospitals in the event of a medical crisis
- control of entry into high-security workplaces and computer systems
- access to air travel as well as to trains, subways, and buses

These are some of the benefits of the smart card.[9] However, the growing use of RFID cards will make it possible for government, police, and intelligence agencies to track the activities, location, communications, and financial transactions of every citizen from cradle to grave.

AN INTERNATIONAL STANDARD FOR PRIVACY

Growing concerns over privacy have motivated representatives of member nations of the European Union (EU) to create an international standard for privacy. The basic rules are as follows:

- All privacy regulations apply to both government and private organizations.
- Data collection should be limited to that which can be obtained legally and with the knowledge and consent of the citizen subject, except where this is impossible or inappropriate (e.g., criminals).
- Data sought on individuals should be limited to the original purpose and kept up to date. The purpose of data collection should be specified, and subsequent use of data should be limited to the original purpose.
- No personal data should be disclosed to others without the consent of the subject or without a court order.
- All personal data must be kept secure using all reasonable precautions.
- All citizens should be able to access, review, and challenge inaccurate data held in databases.

- The government agency controller of the database should be legally and criminally accountable for abiding by these privacy principles.
- The policies and practices of organizations holding databases on individuals should reveal the information to those who legally inquire.
- Private data collected by EU member corporations and states may not be transmitted to organizations in nations that do not have privacy regulations equal to those of the European Union.[10]

The introduction of similar legislation in America, Canada, and other democratic nations could provide significant protection against the abuse of our privacy. The Organization of Economic Cooperation and Development (OECD) is an international group of twenty-nine developed nations from North America, Europe, and Asia that has suggested the creation of powerful, binding privacy standards for both governments and businesses.[11]

The reality is that the growing attacks on our personal security are rapidly overwhelming the proposed defenses. One potential solution is to use a smart stored-value card that would allow a person to make a payment while the card restricts the merchant from accessing the purchaser's identity. The card would also prevent merchants and anyone receiving an electronic funds transfer from tracking previous purchases made by that customer. For example, a smart card developed by Mondex International allows customers to transfer funds from their card to a merchant's account to make a purchase. However, when the merchant's bank accepts the transfer of funds to cover purchases made using Mondex cards, the bank is not able to identify the actual purchasers. A similar system is used by Visa International in its Visa cash card. The disposable card does not permit merchants to identify the person who used the card.

WHAT YOU CAN DO

There are hopeful signs that, after years of indifference to the threats to our privacy and financial security, the public is awakening to the heightened dangers posed by new surveillance technologies.

When it was revealed that Intel Corporation had embedded in every

Pentium III chip a secret serial number that would allow the person using the computer to be identified, customers and privacy groups launched a protest.[12] Additionally, Microsoft had embedded a hidden identification number in all documents produced by any computer using Microsoft software. The protests that followed forced the company to provide a free software program that eliminated the identifying number.[13] However, the vast majority of computer users of Microsoft software are unaware of the privacy problem, and most lack the expertise to fix it.

If we are to protect what little privacy we still have, we should encourage a healthy debate about the relative advantages and disadvantages of each new technological development. Citizen involvement and thoughtful protest against the governmental and corporate threats to our privacy can slow down this relentless attack. We need to defend our right to maintain a personal life that is free from outside interference and intrusion.

Still, in violation of constitutional guarantees to the contrary, our society continues to move toward an all-encompassing surveillance society, which is described in the prophecies of the book of Revelation. We will live to see the time when our right to privacy and the freedom to be left alone are nothing more than distant memories.

CHAPTER 2

THE GLOBAL SURVEILLANCE SOCIETY

How Guarding Against Terrorism Is Turned Against You

Threats of war and terrorist attack give rise to governments' violating the rights of citizens and increasing spying efforts. Since the end of World War II, the United States has monitored virtually all of the communications of other nations. Understandably, national governments and major corporations around the world do everything possible to protect the secrecy of their communications.

A Swiss company, Crypto AG, established its reputation on promises to provide absolutely secure communications systems to governments and corporations. Customers purchased the company's expensive encryption systems with the assurance that their communications would be highly encrypted and, thus, totally secure. With its centuries-long reputation for political neutrality and its advanced technology, Switzerland is viewed in a different light from nations such as the United States, Canada, and Great Britain. As a result Crypto AG was able to sell its encryption systems to nations throughout the world, including Russia, Libya, and Iran.

Nations use the encryption systems to send top-secret diplomatic and military messages to government departments, embassies, trade negotiators, intelligence agencies, and spies around the world. However, the company's assurances of security were unfounded. It came to light that the U.S. National Security Agency (NSA) and Germany's intelligence agency, Bundesnachrichtendienst (BND), had secretly embedded a decryption key within the cipher text produced by Crypto AG. This permitted the NSA and several associated Western intelligence agencies to decode the cipher and read secret messages from most of the world's governments and from numerous large international corporations.[1] For at least fifty years throughout the cold war, the NSA was reading top-secret messages of key governments and businesses as easily as if the communications had been transmitted in the open.[2]

In effect, the NSA used its reach and influence to set up its own backdoor access into encryption devices designed and manufactured by private security companies. The NSA, as the largest intelligence agency in the world, will sometimes "offer preferential export treatment" to security companies that compromise supposedly secure encryption codes with "back doors" that allow decryption by entities other than those who are actually party to the communications.[3]

The United States has, in some instances, demanded that allied nations purchase encryption machines from Crypto AG as a condition for receiving U.S. financial aid or military support. Intelligence experts have stated that Pakistan, for instance, was given substantial American military credits on the condition that it use Crypto AG equipment. Other reports have shown that the NSA developed close working relationships with a number of cryptographic companies besides Crypto AG, including Gretag AG (Switzerland), Transvertex (Sweden), and Nokia (Finland), and a few private encryption companies in postcommunist Hungary.[4]

The NSA uses top-secret "black budgets" involving tens of billions of dollars annually to develop surveillance projects to protect the United States' secret communications and to decode the secrets of every other nation on earth, including America's allies. President Ronald Reagan inadvertently revealed the existence of the NSA's interception and decryption capabilities when he justified a retaliatory attack on Libya in response to terrorist attacks on U.S. soldiers in West Germany. Reagan declared that the United States had intercepted secret communications of the Libyan government that proved that Libyan agents planned the 1986 bombing of the La Belle discotheque in West Berlin's Schoeneberg district. Two American soldiers and a Turkish woman were killed in that attack, and another two hundred people were injured.[5]

This admission confirmed America's ability to monitor another nation's supposedly top-secret communications—in this case between Tripoli and secret agents based in the Libyan embassy in East Berlin. In addition, according to reports in the Swiss newspaper *Neue Zurcher Zeitung*, American sources acknowledged having supplied French officials with transcripts of encrypted Iranian messages confirming the participation of Iranian agents Ali Vakili Rad and Massoud Hendi in the assassination in France of Shahpour Bakhtiar, the exiled former Iranian prime minister.[6]

Security agencies such as the NSA, CIA, FBI, and the U.S. State Department use intelligence data accumulated through the backdoor trap in Crypto AG's machines. At the same time, these agencies cooperate with American and other Western corporations involved in the defense industry and in other businesses. Occasionally, U.S. intelligence agencies request that a company allow an operative to impersonate one of the business's employees in an attempt to gain access to an enemy nation's secrets. Naturally there is a quid pro quo so that industrial espionage secrets gathered by the agent are shared with the cooperating businesses.[7]

Like much that is taking place today on the international scene, these things have great prophetic significance. As we approach the battle of Armageddon, the final global conflict between the West and East, the growing use of high-tech surveillance will continue to destroy every bit of privacy that governments, corporations, and individual citizens formerly enjoyed.

YOUR E-MAIL INVITES EAVESDROPPERS

The speed and convenience of e-mail communications have lulled us into a false sense of security. In contrast with a letter that is typed or handwritten and then mailed to a recipient, your e-mail messages are available to intelligence and law enforcement agencies involved in monitoring electronic communications. Most people think of the Internet as simply a vehicle for instantaneous communication, as if sending an e-mail is the same as making a phone call. Without realizing it, millions of people are creating permanent computer records of their life, activities, purchases, and interests that are likely someday to come back to haunt them. Your electronic "data shadow" will follow you for the rest of your life.

Your business and personal e-mails can be intercepted and scanned by NSA and police computers looking for any use of keywords, addresses, names, images, voices, and numeric sequences. Sophisticated computer programs routinely intercept all e-mails sent throughout the world, both personal and business related. Unfortunately, most e-mail interception is virtually undetectable to the party whose privacy has been violated. The NSA can instantaneously translate e-mails in as many as seventy languages. The agency also uses artificial intelligence software that employs voice-recognition programs to search for certain voices.

Several years ago U.S. Justice Department spokesperson Scott Charney defended the government's monitoring of e-mail and other Internet communications. The rationale given was that democratic societies must balance an individual's right to privacy with the nation's need for security from enemy combatants, terror organizations, organized crime, and foreign agents. While he acknowledged that eliminating general surveillance of private communications would be desirable in an ideal world, Charney stated that it would work only "if everyone were law abiding, but they are not."[8]

Losing your right to send private messages—that is, messages that are read only by the intended recipients—leads to far more than simple embarrassment. E-mail users have been shocked when they have lost a promotion, failed in a job search, or found a valued relationship shattered after their personal communications were used against them. After several decades of research on the shadow government and its use of surveillance technologies, I advise you to conduct your e-mail communications as if a police officer or NSA agent were standing behind you, looking over your shoulder.

You may think I'm exaggerating, but I assure you I know of many individuals who have suffered serious reversals when e-mails they assumed were private—and messages they had deleted—later turned up in the hands of someone who used the messages against them. Most Internet users take advantage of free e-mail services offered by major Internet service providers (ISPs), which share your so-called private e-mail messages with law enforcement agencies around the world. Police from any of the 157 nation-states that are members of Interpol can access your e-mails as well as your Internet searches and ordinary Web surfing.

THE THREAT OF THE INTERNET

The number of people who regularly use the Internet more than doubles every year. Approximately forty-five thousand Internet newsgroups host users who share messages, comments, and jokes. Most participants believe their personal messages disappear when the thread of the newsgroup no longer displays the comment. However, a number of computer databases, including Deja News and Internet Archive, search newsgroups and record the messages. Imagine applying for a promotion or a new job and learning that suddenly, without explanation, you are no longer being considered for the position. While you may never learn the real reason, it's possible that the prospective employer searched an Internet archive and discovered inappropriate comments or Web site visits that reflected poorly on your judgment or revealed unpopular opinions.

The founder of Internet Archive, Brewster Kahle, hired more than thirty people to monitor sophisticated search engines, called spiders, that continuously search more than two billion Web sites and Usenet sites and store the information. Over time, they had accumulated three thousand trillion bytes of computer information.[9]

More than a decade ago, Bruce Schneier, coeditor of *The Electronic Privacy Papers* and a consultant on computer encryption, wrote, "The odd thing is, we perceive the Net as a conversation and not as public record, and it turns out to be public record to a larger extent than people are aware of.... You can easily imagine in 20 years a candidate being asked about a conversation he had in a chat room while he was in college. We're becoming a world where everything is recorded."[10]

Who Owns the Internet?

The Internet began as a small communications network designed by the Defense Advanced Research Projects Agency (DARPA), the research branch of the Pentagon, to connect various military bases and university science laboratories working on defense projects. It grew quickly to connect hundreds of thousands of academics, scientists, and researchers. The original intent for the Internet was noncommercial, but by the early 1990s it was transformed into the largest communications system in history. Today hundreds of millions of individuals, corporations, and organizations depend on the Internet for both internal and external communications. This makes it extremely easy for intelligence agencies to monitor billions of communications every day as they search for a particular target or a specific type or category of communication.

A single private corporation established itself as the sole controller, gatekeeper, and virtual toll collector for every individual, business, and organization that wishes to participate on the Web. The U.S. government initially granted this monopoly to a tax-supported organization called the Internet Network Information Center (INIC), operating under the direction of the National Science Foundation. INIC was responsible for issuing domain names for all Web sites and provided that service without charge. Each Web site must possess a unique electronic address, an Internet protocol (IP) address, which pairs a unique numeric address with an easily remembered (and also unique) name. For example, my Web site, www.grantjeffrey.com, is simpler to recall than its actual numeric address, which might be a numeric sequence such as 123.273.486.8.

The U.S. government required that people and entities who wanted to set up a Web site with a unique Internet address ending in any of the well-known suffixes—.com, .edu, .org, .net, or .gov—must register their domain name with INIC. However, in 1993 the government transferred the domain registry function to a private corporation called Network Solutions Inc. (NSI). Many Internet users were outraged when, in September 1995, NSI required that anyone wanting to register a new domain address pay one hundred dollars, with annual address renewals priced at fifty dollars. Not surprisingly, this is a lucrative business. In 1995, NSI was acquired by Science Applications International Corporation (SAIC), a privately held company with more than twenty thousand employees working in 450 locations throughout the world and with revenue of almost nine billion dollars in 2007.

The most disturbing aspect of this exclusive arrangement is the implied control. SAIC, the ninth-largest defense contractor in the United States, is operated by individuals who have worked for decades within the Pentagon and various intelligence organizations. Over the years SAIC's board of directors has included the former head of the NSA, former directors of the CIA, former secretaries of the Department of Defense, and a former chief of research and development at the Pentagon.

Why is the U.S. intelligence community so intent on controlling the key entry points into the major communication system that links the world's governments, corporations, and billions of citizens? Organizations and national security agencies that are able to control and monitor the Internet are in a position to access billions of daily communications. Virtually every e-mail, chat room conversation, Web search, or other Internet communication can be analyzed by intelligence authorities. Presently—fortunately—the United States is a democracy where the existence of political checks and balances, together with the judicial system, provides some measure of confidence that major privacy violations will be limited. However, it's obvious that in the hands of any future dictatorial government, this surveillance technology could make it almost impossible to escape the control of totalitarian police and security forces. In chapter 5, we will explore the capabilities of the global surveillance system, known as Project Echelon, that can monitor almost all electronic communications on earth.

Google Is Interested in You Personally

Google quickly became the largest Internet search engine in the world. Its vast subterranean hard-drive storage facilities can record and store billions of e-mail messages and the more than 330 million daily Google searches. Google has stated that it stores its users' e-mail messages and the history of their customer's Internet searches for eighteen months.[11]

Google and other search engines offer research services to its users for free, but the reality is that Google makes billions of dollars annually by revealing information it gains from deep mining its users' Internet searches and e-mails. Google has built a highly intrusive picture of your life, health, relationships, finances, employment, reading interests, and political and religious interests. Search engine corporations such as Google sell that information to retailers and other institutions that wish to precisely target their commercial, political, or religious communications at those individuals most likely to respond positively.[12]

Sharing Your Financial Records

Many of us grew up in families that closely guarded all financial information, considering this the most private topic of all. A person's salary and the financial details of one's neighbors and fellow employees were never discussed. Only the loan officer or a teller at your local bank knew details of your financial history, and bank officers were committed to confidentiality. Even if you grew up in such a world, you don't live there any longer.

Today any inquisitive neighbor, fellow employee, boss, friend, or enemy can access the most intimate details of your financial life, credit history, real-estate holdings, mortgage information, criminal record, court cases, educational background, and so forth. The federal Freedom of Information Act requires that government records and documents be made available to the public to ensure transparency. The Web makes these records easily accessible to people from the convenience of their home or office. Details of your financial history, even from many years ago, are available to anyone who has enough curiosity about you to access your records online.

Some government agencies release to the public personal and financial data they have collected from private citizens. For example, the FBI has responded to the demands of citizens who want access to once-secret FBI files. Anyone with a computer can access the FBI's Web site (http://foia.fbi.gov), where they can read thousands of unclassified or formerly classified government documents, including files on Elvis Presley, Frank Sinatra, and John F. Kennedy Jr. FBI files are available on such diverse topics as aviator Amelia Earhart, who was lost at sea, and the infamous Project Blue Book on UFO sightings.[13]

Despite the obvious dangers posed by your use of the Internet, it is a tool that is virtually indispensable for research, business, and communication. While there is a growing concern among academics and intellectuals about the risks to our privacy, the technology is so embedded in conducting business and keeping in touch with friends, family members, and colleagues, not to mention researching information and making purchases, that its increasing use is irreversible.

The apostle John made a remarkable prophecy almost two thousand years ago. He indicated that a future world dictator would develop a comprehensive system of police control that would make it impossible for anyone, "small and great, rich and poor, free and bond," to avoid being subject to the evil ruler's control (Revelation 13:16). The development in our generation of unprecedented systems of communication, along with the abuse of this technology by intelligence and police agencies, is a significant indication that we are living in the last days.

CHAPTER 3

EVERY MOVEMENT AND PURCHASE IS TRACKED

Welcome to the Pervasive Threat of RFID Chips

The most intrusive consumer surveillance technology introduced in recent years is the radio frequency identification (RFID) chip, which is implanted in billions of individual consumer products. Most people are not aware that a microscopic RFID chip hidden in an article of clothing, a book, or any other consumer product can enable the retailer, the product's manufacturer, and even an intelligence or police agency to track the product and you, the purchaser. If you buy a product with an embedded RFID chip, you can be tracked from the store's checkout counter, where your identity is recorded from your credit or debit card. The time that you leave the store is recorded at the store's exit by reading the RFID chip embedded in the purchased item. And your movements long after you leave the store can be tracked by anyone with an RFID reader, as long as you have the chipped product with you. If you take the book to a coffee shop or wear the shirt to work or keep the DVD in your car, RFID readers can track the presence of that consumer item (and, by extension, your presence) within a certain distance from each reading device.

RFID EXPLAINED

At the heart of the RFID system is the Electronic Product Code (EPC), which established a way to identify every individual item manufactured in any nation of the world. Each item is assigned a unique ninety-six-bit alphanumeric EPC that identifies the nation of manufacture, type of product, manufacturer's name, retailer, and other identification data.[1]

The EPC system replaces the universal bar code system, known as the Universal Product Code (UPC). The RFID-EPC system adds to each physical item and manufacturer identifier a unique number that can be used to identify the purchaser. This unique serial number is assigned to you when you purchase the product, linking you alone to that particular transaction and the particular item that you take with you when you leave the store. Astonishingly, this system applies a unique ID number to every one of the billions of products purchased, even individual cans of Diet Pepsi or a personal grooming product. RFID tags are potentially able to identify and monitor more than 268 million individual manufacturers, with each corporation having more than one million separate products.[2] The older UPC bar code system can identify only a hundred thousand separate manufacturers and types of products, not every individual, physical item produced. In addition, the scanner needs to be within twelve inches of the bar code.

Procter and Gamble–Gillette and the Massachusetts Institute of Technology invested in developing the Electronic Product Code utilizing RFID chips. A new data standard called Physical Markup Language (PML) identifies the type of product and any pertinent data related to it. A further step in the system is the Object Naming Service (ONS), which links the EPC with the PML, creating a unique RFID number that will enable corporate databases to locate any particular item (and ultimately the individual who purchased it) anywhere in the world. Those who study manufacturing and retailing operations can visualize a time in the near future when a global RFID system will be used to identify and track every physical item produced and sold on earth.[3]

RFID Chips in Your Possession

By 2004 more than sixty thousand American corporations were introducing RFID chips into every item they manufactured and distributed globally.[4] Gillette was a major early adopter. In 2003 Gillette ordered more than five hundred million RFID chips, which were embedded in their products, including the very popular Mach 3 razors. At the time of this writing, more than one and a half billion RFID chips are inserted in products each year, and there is no legal requirement for companies to inform consumers that a product contains an embedded RFID chip.

Wal-Mart, the world's leading retailer using RFID product tagging, invested $250 million in the introduction of RFID technology. By requiring their one hundred top manufacturers and key distributors to embed all high-tech products, including consumer electronics, with RFID tags, Wal-Mart forced virtually the entire U.S. consumer-products industry to adopt RFID technology. The program is used to monitor Wal-Mart's vast inventory from manufacturer to shipper to the particular shelf in a particular store on which a particular product sits.[5]

Steven Van Fleet, program director of e-packaging and silent commerce at International Paper, has said that as much as 7 percent of products are stolen or misplaced during distribution and that RFID chips assist in cutting down on theft and fraud.[6] The Anti-Counterfeiting Coalition estimates that trademark counterfeiting, another major problem in the retail distribution chain, robs U.S. companies of $200 billion in revenue annually. Smart tags could reduce these losses significantly.[7] Those who promote RFID technology claim that "theft will be drastically reduced because items will report when they are stolen, their smart tags also serving as a homing device toward their exact location."[8]

Public libraries have been enthusiastic early adopters of RFID technology. Libraries place RFID chips in the spines and covers of books to enable the institutions to track, inventory, and possibly recover lost or stolen books. Unfortunately, the existence of RFID chips within a library's book inventory makes it much easier for authorities to monitor the type of reading you do and the topics that interest you. Whether you are reading about religion, radical political movements, bomb making, anarchy, cooking, or history, your reading habits will be known by the authorities.

The United States Postal Service plans to embed every postage stamp with a tiny RFID chip that would enable postal authorities to track all stamp-bearing letters and parcels from point to point across the nation. RFID-embedded stamps will enable postal officials to easily monitor all mail sent to or from any targeted organization.

Owning Up to the Threat

IBM, a major early promoter of RFID technology, has admitted that the technology has the potential to be misused to such a degree that every citizen's privacy could be lost. Remarkably, IBM's patent application for RFID technology acknowledged this inherent danger: "The widespread use of RFID tags on merchandise such as clothing would make it possible for the locations of people, animals, and objects to be tracked on a global scale—a privacy invasion of Orwellian proportions."[9]

IBM was referring to George Orwell's prophetic novel *1984,* where every action taken and every word spoken by every citizen was recorded and evaluated by governmental and law enforcement officials. While many observers reject the conclusion that RFID chips might be used to conduct surveillance of an individual, IBM and others have made it clear that this technology, in the wrong hands, can identify and track the communications and travel of a targeted individual. The monitoring agent would be unknown to the person being tracked. It could conceivably be a governmental or private investigative agency.

Since a tracking device is required to read the signal from the chip, you might wonder how any interested party would be able to track your movements through an embedded RFID chip. The answer is that RFID scanners are located in places you would never suspect. Scanners can be hidden in the doors, floors, and walls of the stores you enter and the offices, banks, and airports you visit. Without your knowledge, entities such as retailers, consumer product companies, the government, the police, and intelligence agencies will be able to track your location and your daily activities.

IBM developed a program known as Margaret, designed to embed RFID scanners in the doors and floors of thousands of banks and other financial institutions. Wealthy customers are given passbooks and loyalty cards that contain RFID chips, which alert the bank's customer identification system as soon as the valued customer enters the building. This allows members of a consumer relations team to provide a heads-up to bank managers and automatically brings up the customer's account information on the bank's computer system. With all of this information at his or her disposal, a teller can greet the customer by name, as if the customer were a long-lost friend.[10]

Most passive RFID chips can be read by a device when the chip passes within seventy-five feet of the scanner. When an RFID chip comes within reading range, a radio signal activates the passive RFID chip to transmit its unique ID number as well as any other electronic information that is programmed into the chip. More recently, electronics manufacturers have developed an active RFID chip that has its own microscopic battery (less than .04 inches thick) that can be read from a distance of a mile or even farther.

An Israeli company, Power Paper Ltd., has been working with International Paper Company to introduce a tiny, flat, flexible, battery-powered RFID chip that will send the EPC ID number a considerable distance, allowing it to be read even by a satellite. International Paper suggests that more than half a billion microscopic RFID chips will be implanted in a great variety of consumer products within a few years, including products as diverse as food packaging and consumer electronics.[11]

THE CONSTANT THREAT TO ORDINARY CITIZENS

A law-abiding citizen might wonder why he should be concerned about this technology, even if the book he is reading or the clothes he is wearing contain a tiny chip that is sending a signal that reveals his location and movements. You should bear in mind that an RFID chip provides much more information than your location. It also transmits a unique ID number that is linked solely to you and is tied to your credit or debit card account, linked to your purchases, and makes available other details about your life.

Over time as you buy more products that contain RFID chips, marketers and retailers (and intelligence agencies) will have virtually unlimited information about you. Depending on who gains access to this data, you could be secretly monitored in all your personal activities by unknown and sinister outsiders.

The growing threat to your privacy from RFID technology can be summarized in three areas:

- Retail and manufacturing companies want to monitor and track all your purchases and activities so they can tailor future marketing and advertising strategies to more effectively reach you and motivate you to become a repeat customer.
- RFID could be used far beyond manufacturers and sellers of consumer products. The international allied government intelligence agencies (Echelon) can easily gain access to this data to extend their exhaustive surveillance efforts to include your movements, location, and communications. (We will explore Project Echelon in chapter 5.
- The third group that could easily misuse RFID technology is organized crime, often operating across international boundaries and on the Internet. Criminal groups that gain access to RFID readers can identify vulnerable targets based on ID codes and information on that individual's recent purchases. Beyond helping to select future targets for traditional crime rings, RFID technology could ultimately make electronic identity theft much more effective and efficient.

The governments of the United States, Canada, and the European Union have not established regulations, reporting requirements, or serious limitations for the use of RFID data acquired by product manufacturers without the consumer's knowledge or approval. Without giving notice to the customer, virtually every individual item sold will be identifiable through its EPC number.[12] Buyer beware, indeed.

Multiple-Application RFID Cards

The banking industry is advocating the adoption of RFID smart cards for use as a multiapplication card. In certain ways such a development could help protect consumers against fraud and identity theft, which are prevalent in large measure due to our reliance on credit and debit cards. Criminals can cause a great deal of harm by acquiring a credit card slip with your name and credit card number on it. Once in possession of that information, criminals can use your credit record to apply for new credit cards. Unfortunately for honest citizens, desktop publishing programs, together with inexpensive scanners and powerful laser printers, permit anyone with good computer skills to create legitimate-looking checks, educational transcripts, and real-estate documents that are used to defraud companies, government agencies, and individuals.

Proponents of the multiple-application RFID smart card maintain that such a card would provide a higher level of security than current cards and other personal documents. It would replace your driver's license, car registration, auto insurance card, medical insurance file, credit and debit cards, prepaid subway and bus cards, and cards to grant you access to secure areas and possibly even to your personal computer. The multiapplication card is designed with individually encrypted digital keys that allow outside access only from the specific business, agency, or institution (bank, driver's license bureau, etc.) that can establish a legitimate need for encoded data. Unauthorized attempts to access the data on a stolen smart card are blocked. One security system causes the smart card to permanently shut down all future card functions if an unauthorized individual attempts to penetrate the encoded security system. After only three unsuccessful attempts at passwords, the card's security shuts down all functions.

The U.S. General Services Administration (GSA) ran a test involving four hundred employees using a multiapplication smart card with an embedded Java computer software system. This card has a computer chip on one side and a magnetic strip with a written signature on the other. The magnetic strip is used at automated-teller machines (ATMs) and retail stores. The card provided the four hundred employees access to their office in Vienna, Virginia. (These cards can be imprinted with biometric information, including fingerprints and voice or iris recognition, to allow access to high-security areas.) The card also acted as a credit/debit card, a calling card for telecommunications, and a digital signature card for authenticating secure work-related communications. It also could be used by employees to board flights when on official business and flying on certain American Airlines planes.

Smart Cards That Replace Cash

Even in parts of the world that lag behind in technology, smart cards are already being used for identification and for replacing cash. In Reynosa, Mexico, low-wage workers who may not have bank accounts often are robbed when they carry home their wages. MetaCo LLC, a payroll company based in Rochester, New York, developed a novel solution. They created a smart card called MetaCard. Each worker has his or her fingerprints scanned and electronically encoded in the MetaCard, preventing anyone from stealing and using the card. The employee can use the card as a timecard at work by swiping it in the smart card reader as he or she enters and exits the factory. Each week the company electronically deposits the worker's wages into the card's memory chip, allowing the employee to use the card at the factory cafeteria to access cash or to automatically deposit unused funds in an interest-bearing bank account.[13]

Cash is already being replaced in most countries of the world. Studies suggest that less than 3 percent of the "money" in North America exists in the form of coins and paper currency. In most cases the rest of the money is represented by computer digits and accounts in bank computers. We are already an almost cashless society, with the exception of small economic transactions, usually under fifty dollars in value. Most studies suggest that 97 percent of financial transactions globally are cashless. This is where smart cards are most likely to have their greatest impact. As people become more comfortable with smart cards, the use of paper currency and coins will continue to decline. The same will be true as smart cards gradually replace credit cards and debit cards.

However, the widespread use of smart cards may cause a very real danger to your privacy. While RFID cards provide a high level of security against traditional forms of fraud and larceny, the technology is vulnerable to attack from sophisticated technology utilized by the NSA and its equivalent agencies in other countries.

The multiapplication smart card could give hackers access to computer-linked databases holding vast amounts of confidential information on every citizen. If a highly knowledgeable criminal, private investigator, or intelligence operative acquired access to the computer database holding the secret records connected to each citizen's smart card, that person would be inside the encrypted security system and able to copy vital personal information.

Another concern is that illegal access to this information could be used to target religious or political groups. Data from smart cards could allow militant opponents or enemy agents to track the movements and identify the meeting locations of adherents to a rival religion or political group, giving them the information they would need to plan and launch an attack. This same danger applies to government agencies that, in the future, might take action against political opponents or adherents to a religion or belief system that opposes the policies of the government.

Even Your Cash Will Be Tracked

Many who are troubled by these developments believe the solution is to live "off the grid." One of the simplest ways to begin is to use cash for your purchases and other financial transactions. However, even the assumed anonymity of using cash is under attack. Both Japan and the European Union have proposed adding microscopic RFID chips to their new currency, enabling monetary authorities to track the movement of banknotes as they travel through the economy. In the near future it will be possible for a criminal with an RFID reader to drive down a street and "read" the amount of money being carried by pedestrians and other motorists.

The European Central Bank is developing RFID tags to be embedded in the fibers of all new euro banknotes. The presence of a hidden RFID tag in every banknote will allow banks and government agencies to record the history of each individual bill. The ability to track and record detailed information about where every euro banknote has been means that governments, the police, and intelligence agencies will possess an extremely intrusive tool to track your every financial transaction.[14]

When RFID devices are embedded in all American and Canadian banknotes, the privacy, anonymity, and freedom that cash currently provides will be eliminated. This is particularly sobering in light of the Bible's warning in Revelation 13:16–17 that the Antichrist will control all commerce, including an individual's ability to buy and sell.

YOUR CAR, CELL PHONE, AND DRIVER'S LICENSE BETRAY YOU

The use of RFID chips is becoming so pervasive that even if you never bought a new consumer item, used a credit or debit card, or shopped online, you could still be tracked through the use and possession of common things such as a cell phone, an automobile, and even your driver's license. Many Americans, especially those living in states bordering Canada and Mexico, will be offered the chance to carry a driver's license that will contain an embedded RFID chip that will identify them to everyone from local police, to the Border Patrol, to Homeland Security if they get within thirty feet of an international border crossing. In 2008 the state of New York issued driver's licenses with RFID chips that, when scanned at a distance, enable New York drivers to travel between the United States and Canada, as well as Mexico, without a U.S. passport. The New York State Enhanced Driver License will allow New York residents to board ships traveling to Bermuda and Caribbean nations without showing a passport.[15]

Most citizens have no idea how this technology could expose them to identity theft, fraud, and the silent surveillance of their private lives. Once someone with an RFID reader detects the ID number from the chip embedded in a driver's license, that anonymous person (often a criminal) has possession of another person's identity as well as the unique ID number assigned only to that person. This could seriously compromise the individual's security.

Anyone with an RFID reader who detects your unique ID number and who has access to the massive consumer database of RFID numbers might be able to identify your presence in an airport or anywhere else by monitoring the radio frequency emitted from your driver's license. Other ordinary activities, such as purchasing gas with your credit or debit card (while carrying your driver's license), will allow outsiders to cross-reference the RFID chip in your driver's license with your credit card number. They will know not only your buying habits but also your location, your movements, and your preferences in eating out and entertainment. Over time they would be able to track the patterns of your daily habits, your route to work, your after-work commitments, and so forth.

Starting in 2000, steps were taken toward augmenting driver's licenses to make them serve as multiuse ID cards, with additional functions built in. Every state in the United States was required to adopt a type of driver's license that contains the driver's Social Security number, which "can be read visually or by electronic means."[16] The long-range plan is to convert all existing driver's licenses into national ID cards, making it possible for the federal government to track virtually all citizens whenever and wherever they travel. It is important to remember that the U.S. government promised the American people in 1932 that the Social Security number would never be used for purposes of national citizen identification.

Many states are beginning to modify driver's licenses so they can be used as RFID smart cards. Each driver's license will be equipped both with a computer RFID chip and a magnetic strip, with biometric information on the owner. Personal information embedded in the license will include a digitized fingerprint, voiceprint, iris scan, and/or DNA print. These smart cards will enable police and intelligence agencies to track all your future activities. For example, the smart card driver's license soon to be introduced in New Jersey will have the ability to track bridge and highway tolls, credit card records, medical visits, and even late-book fines in the state's library system.

Millions of North Americans already use EZ Pass and similar electronic systems to automatically pay tolls on roads and bridges. Millions of drivers use Mobil Speed Pass but are blissfully unaware that RFID technology is transmitting their ID whenever they pass a tollbooth with an RFID reader. EZ Pass and other toll transmitters allow authorities to monitor your travel, your speed, and location when you use a tollway.

Phones That Double as Credit Cards

Cell phones are so widely used that many people no longer have a landline in their home. Now cell phones are about to replace even your credit and debit cards. Manufacturers of high-end mobile phones are starting to add an RFID chip that allows phone users to buy consumer products by holding the RFID-equipped telephone near a store's cash register. An RFID reader in the store scans a number from the chip in the phone and automatically debits the amount of the purchase from the customer's credit or debit card account.[17]

The credit card giant Barclaycard, which introduced the UK's first credit cards in 1966, has embraced RFID-equipped mobile phones that are used to make purchases. Barclaycard also developed an RFID credit card that can interface with a store's computer system to enable you to complete a purchase without taking your wallet out of your pocket or purse. An RFID reader in the store can scan the credit card number without a cashier's having to swipe the card through a reader or to use a bar code scanner.

The introduction of smart phones that contain RFID chips goes far beyond making it more convenient to shop. The chips in high-end phones will accelerate the invasion of your privacy. Any user of a smart phone can be tracked, because the RFID chip in the phone emits a radio signal. You may have seen a television ad for the iPhone that will show you the physical location of your friends so you can join them wherever they are. That means the police, a government agency, or a criminal could likewise locate your friends or you.

The Spy-Chipped Car in Your Future

The government has proposed that new cars manufactured in the United States be equipped with RFID chips and global positioning transceivers. These additions will enable auto manufacturers to track the cars they build from the moment they leave the factory, are transported to the dealer, and are sold and driven off the dealer's lot. An 802.11 wireless radio frequency device in the car would upload the location, time, and up-to-date vehicle data whenever the car passes near a wireless radio receiver hot spot.[18]

Any police or intelligence agency using this technology could easily monitor the exact location and direction of travel of any RFID-equipped car. The Federal Communications Commission has reserved a radio frequency range specifically for applications such as those needed for automobile RFID chips.

STEPS TOWARD ISSUING A PERSONAL ID NUMBER

In 2008 the U.S. State Department introduced a new passport that contained an RFID chip. The rationale behind this is that a chip-embedded passport enables immigration and customs officers to more efficiently process the entrance of U.S. citizens into the country.

The International Civil Aviation Organization (ICAO), an agency of the United Nations, demanded in 2003 that all UN member states begin establishing passport standards that use the RFID chip. In the near future virtually all international travelers will be tracked and monitored by RFID devices. Nations that have since adopted the use of RFID chips embedded within their passports include the United States, the United Kingdom, Australia, New Zealand, China, Japan, and most member nations of the European Union.

The newer generation of RFID passports, initiated in August 2007, contain advanced security features that are more protected than the original electronic passport. New security features include a "randomized unique identification" system that creates a different ID number every time the chip is accessed when

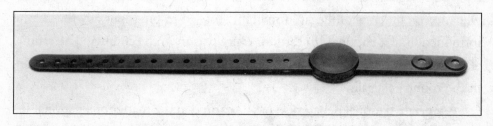

An effective device to monitor a select population. This bracelet containing a computer chip was used by the U.S. Army to monitor 50,000 Haitian refugees.

a citizen approaches a customs station. It also contains a digital signature that acts as a check on the integrity of the RF number and helps determine if the passport's data has been altered. Finally, a metallic insert in the spine and front cover of the passport is designed to block radio signals when the passport cover is closed. (Several tests indicated, however, that radio signals revealing the RFID number can still be read when the passport cover is closed. One solution is to carry your passport inside a foil-equipped wallet that blocks the radio signal.)[19]

In 2008, in response to the reluctance of millions of Americans to apply for passports to travel to Canada or Mexico, the State Department introduced through the Department of Homeland Security a US-VISIT program to facilitate travel for Americans to those two countries. The new travel identity PASS (People Access Security Service) cards are an alternate travel document to the traditional passport. Every American citizen entering the United States must carry either a regular U.S. passport or an alternative travel document such as the PASS card. The PASS identity document is a limited-use wallet-size card that is readable up to a distance of seventy-five feet from an RFID reader. In that way immigration and customs officers can capture information on the person entering the country. His or her photograph and other personal data is automatically displayed on a computer screen at the border crossing.[20]

A National ID Card for Every Citizen

The national debate over illegal immigration and controlling the nation's borders has given rise to a discussion about developing a more effective method for identifying and monitoring the movements of all persons entering the country—both legally and otherwise. Fear that the United States is being overwhelmed by millions of illegal immigrants has led to proposals advocating the introduction of a national ID card for every person in the country. The rationale is that a national ID card would enable authorities to identify those who are in the country illegally.

A separate national debate also has a bearing on the matter of a national ID card. Talk of a universal healthcare plan returned to the national agenda following the election in 2008 of Barack Obama as president. If such a plan is adopted by Congress, it will require that every U.S. citizen carry an ID card.

Officials argue that a national ID card would serve other essential purposes, such as helping to guard against welfare cheats. With one authorized ID card, those who would otherwise double-dip by collecting benefits in two or more jurisdictions, or by using a fake ID, would be prevented from doing so. Another use for the card would be to track down deadbeat parents seeking to evade payment of court-ordered child or spousal support. Eventually, a uniform national ID card could replace a variety of existing identification papers, such as passports, driver's licenses, voter registration cards, and even birth certificates.

The key requirement for an effective national ID system would be the implementation of a new smart card. Each citizen would be given a unique identification number, permitting government databases to identify and link all relevant data concerning that individual to a single ID number. Currently, data is scattered among thousands of separate state and federal databases, as well as corporate databases. Acceptance of the number would be enforced by a government requirement that services could not be accessed without using one's ID number. For example, a citizen would have to submit an identification document with a unique assigned number to receive healthcare, or the healthcare provider would not be paid.

This unique identification number would allow all your private medical data to be collated into a central, comprehensive computer file without your knowledge or approval. Such information could be accessed by a party that is researching your background and personal history—including potential employers, insurers, or others who have an interest in your health and medical history. The Patient Protection Act (HR 4250), passed by the U.S. House of Representatives in 1998, allows any company that records personal medical records on U.S. citizens to gather, exchange, and distribute the records, as long as the information will be used only for "healthcare operations" (a phrase that is not defined in the act).

In China, the move toward a national ID program is much further along.

China has undertaken the largest RFID program in the world, at a cost of six billion dollars. The purpose is to force the adoption of RFID chips by every one of the more than 1.3 billion Chinese citizens. The Chinese government has chosen to encode a staggering amount of sensitive data within the new national ID cards. For example, my sources reveal that Chinese national ID cards will include a citizen's full name, address, health information, reproductive history, employment history, religion, ethnicity, landlord's identity, and much more. This massive accumulation and control of citizens' personal information is only one small element in a comprehensive population surveillance society proposal that the Chinese government has embraced.

PREPARE FOR YOUR OWN ID IMPLANT

At this point do you have any remaining doubts regarding the underlying motives of those who promote RFID technology? The surveillance system made possible by RFID chips goes far beyond anything conceived by Adolf Hitler or Joseph Stalin. Consider a quote from the associate director of the Auto-ID Center, the major promoter of the universal commercial adoption of RFID technology: "The Auto-ID Center has a clear vision—to create a world where every object—from jumbo jets to sewing needles—is linked to the Internet. Compelling as this vision is, it is only achievable if the center's system is adopted by everyone elsewhere. Success will be nothing less than global adoption."[21]

The philosopher C. P. Snow warned in a 1971 *New York Times* article, "Technology…is a queer thing. It brings you great gifts with one hand, and it stabs you in the back with the other."[22]

The U.S. Food and Drug Administration (FDA) has given initial approval to the use of subcutaneous (beneath the skin) RFID chips to enable hospitals and medical staff to monitor patient medical records. And it won't be long before possession of a national RFID-equipped ID card will be required for a person to conduct many daily functions. However, having to carry a card is inconvenient, and a card can be easily lost, damaged, or stolen. That is one reason for growing support behind an implanted ID chip. A subcutaneous chip could never be lost, and it could be stolen only through a surgical procedure. Several companies have created a miniature computer-chip radio transponder that can be safely and painlessly implanted beneath the skin. Such a chip could be injected at the same time as a vaccine or be implanted on its own.

The concept of placing a computer chip beneath every person's skin has great advantages for banks and the security agencies of the government. The chip would contain all your personal information, as well as biometric identification such as an iris scan or voiceprint. A surgically implanted chip could assist in the radio frequency monitoring of inmates on parole from prison but still under house arrest. It could also provide their precise location by Global Positioning System (GPS) satellites. In addition, GPS devices could ensure the safe identification and continual tracking of patients under medical care, such as those with Alzheimer's. If someone suffered a heart attack or other medical emergency, an implanted GPS device would enable paramedics to quickly locate the victim.

Despite these advantages, the widespread use of implanted chips would eliminate our privacy. The history of surveillance technology suggests that the information initially collected for innocent purposes will ultimately be used for other purposes, and even against our best interests.

The average citizen may find this disturbing, but there is already a growing tendency for government and business to use RFID chips to provide foolproof identification for pets and livestock and for special medical situations. Secure military installations and high-security financial facilities have already implanted RFID chips in key employees to ensure security.

PROPHECIES OF ID IMPLANTS?

Some two thousand years before anyone seriously considered the technology needed to implement a national or global ID system, the prophet John described just such a thing. He prophesied a global totalitarian system that would monitor the choices of individuals and rob them of their freedom. "No man might buy or sell, save he that had the mark, or the name of the beast, or

the number of his name…. [H]is number is Six hundred threescore and six"
(Revelation 13:17–18).

Imagine a person living in the first century trying to picture how such a system could be developed and implemented. But today, John's prophecy does not
seem at all far-fetched. With a unique ID code included in every RFID chip,
virtually every person can already be monitored and tracked. And many people
around the world are using RFID technology to conduct business and complete
financial transactions. A report from Spain told about bars in Barcelona that
offered to implant RFID chips in their regular customers. That way VIP customers could buy drinks without having to use cash.[23]

The rapidly expanding use of this technology is far from just a novelty. All
of those who reject Jesus Christ's offer of salvation will be left behind on earth
to face seven years of global terror. This period of unprecedented suffering and
upheaval, known as the Tribulation, will be controlled by the Antichrist.

In this final great crisis, everyone will face a life-and-death decision. The
Antichrist will claim to be god on earth, and his partner, the False Prophet, will
demand that everyone worship the Antichrist as god. Every person on earth will
be forced to declare allegiance to him by accepting the Mark of the Beast—666.
The Word of God warns that anyone who chooses to accept the 666 mark will
be damned forever. However, the Bible promises that anyone who rejects the
Antichrist and his mark and instead worships Christ will be saved.

The prophet John saw all these things in a vision. Today we are seeing in
our generation the technological developments that can make possible the 666
Mark of the Beast system.

CHAPTER 4

HOW YOUR PRIVATE LIFE GOES PUBLIC

*Who Else Is Listening to Your Calls
and Reading Your E-Mail?*

Imagine your postal carrier opening up and making a copy of the contents of every piece of your incoming mail before putting it in your mailbox. And picture him doing the same with your outgoing mail before he deposits it at the post office. He creates an archived copy of every letter you write, every bill you pay, every product you order, and every inquiry you make by mail.

But it doesn't end there. Your postal carrier creates additional copies of your outgoing mail and makes them widely available so that masses of strangers can also read them. Suddenly your private life, your personal finances, your purchases, and the topics you research are known to intelligence agencies, the police, the government, your employer, your fellow employees, and even curious people living in your neighborhood.

Would that disturb you?

Just in case that scenario doesn't anger you, here's another one to consider. Every time you make a call on your cell phone, any agency that has reason to wonder where you are can use your phone to locate you. Beyond that, every phone number you call or text you send or receive is recorded, and the records are maintained for years. Even your travel, whether by public transportation or in a private vehicle, is monitored while you carry your cell phone.

In the United States because the Constitution guarantees certain rights to citizens—including the right to keep our personal matters private—we have assumed that our secrets are ours to protect, that only those whom we choose to tell will know about our private matters.

That is no longer the case.

The details of your life are on record, and you no longer have any control over who has access to those secrets. Your travel habits and hotel destinations; the books, movies, and music you borrow from the library; your movie rentals; your choices on pay-TV; traffic tickets; medical tests; and almost every purchase you make using a credit or debit card—all of these details are recorded and permanently archived. Your records are stored on corporate databases as well as on U.S. Treasury Department databases, and the information is accessible to a surprising number of people, businesses, and government agencies—the federal government as well as law enforcement and even intelligence agencies of other national governments.

BIG BROTHER *ALREADY* KNOWS

It would be easy for law-abiding citizens to feel they have no secrets that could be damaging to them. But consider this: enormous amounts of extremely revealing private information are permanently "on file" on the Internet, and virtually anyone can access the data. As a result of agreements with Interpol (International Criminal Police Organization), even sensitive intelligence files are available to numerous police agencies around the globe. A large number of corporate information marketers, such as international credit agencies, barter with or pay foreign corporations to obtain information that previously was assumed to be private. This means that untold numbers of strangers now know all about your lifestyle, purchases, tax records, and real-estate holdings.

Being under continual surveillance is fundamentally altering our way of life. Our privacy is being eliminated by the development and implementation of intrusive surveillance technologies. Recent technological developments have produced capabilities that are far more thorough and effective than the spy capabilities of the totalitarian government imagined by George Orwell in his prophetic novel *1984*, written as a warning near the beginning of the cold war.

ID Chips on a Ring

Here is just one of the remarkable advances in security technology. The Java iButton, developed by Dallas Semiconductor Corporation, is a computer chip contained in a tiny stainless-steel case. The miniature container can be worn

A digital iButton ring from Dallas Semiconductor. It can be used to access ATMs, a personal computer, and public transportation and to purchase items from certain vending machines.

like jewelry, as a charm attached to a bracelet, key fob, watch, or your clothing. Millions of iButton computer chips are used to communicate with, access, and control desktop, laptop, and handheld computers. When you touch the iButton to a receptor device such as a computer, information is transferred at the rate of 142,000 bits per second. This device can contain personal identification and biometric information as well as financial data or medical information. In Mexico, customers simply touch an iButton ring to a "Blue Dot" receptor on a gas pump, and money is deducted from their bank account to pay for the gasoline. In Argentina and Brazil, iButtons are used by millions to pay at parking meters. Millions of commuters in Turkey use the iButton to pay for tickets to ride the mass-transit system.

This type of technology is likely to be used globally to increase security and avoid the need for cash. The disadvantage is that there will be a permanent computer record of every transaction you conduct using an iButton. The recorded data will include the time and place of your travel, a point of embarkation, and your destination. Your location, movements, itinerary, routines, and life habits will become an open book to any interested party.

Broadcasting Your Location

At an airport in Brussels, as a businessman hurried toward a boarding gate, he paused to phone his secretary, entering his credit card number into his cell phone to enable her to make some purchases for him. He was unaware that cyberthieves intercepted his call, using portable radio scanners, and obtained his phone number and credit card numbers. In the following days the man's credit card number and phone number were used to make purchases and numerous phone calls to the criminals' colleagues around the world. This scenario illustrates a crime that any of us could fall victim to.

Most users of analog cellular phones are unaware of the ease with which radio scanners can intercept radio frequencies to listen in on private calls. Public figures including the late Princess Diana, Prince Charles, and Newt Gingrich, former Speaker of the House of Representatives, were embarrassed to discover that their cell phone calls were intercepted and made public, revealing their secrets to the world.

Newer digital cell phones use encryption techniques that make the interception of calls by scanners almost impossible for the average phone hacker. Yet there are new scanning devices sold by high-tech surveillance shops that enable a person to crack most digital encryptions. While more-secure encryption systems may be developed, at the present time it would be prudent to refrain from discussing any confidential or financial information over your cell phone. You never know who is listening.

In addition to the threat of having your phone calls intercepted, simply carrying your cell phone with you announces where you are. Congress requires that all manufacturers of cell phones design their products so that wireless phone service providers are able to pinpoint any 911 caller's location within four hundred feet.[1] Your cellular carrier can triangulate your exact location by calculating your distance from three cell towers. As long as your cell phone battery has power, it is sending out a signal that is picked up by cell towers.

Phone companies keep such records on hand for years. If the police or an intelligence agency needed to, it could determine the precise location of your phone at a certain time on a certain date. A private source told me that this technology was used by the Los Angeles Police to locate O. J. Simpson when he fled from his home in the now-famous white Ford Bronco, which later was involved in a slow-speed police chase. You might have seen it on television.

Surveillance Controls at National Borders

When you drive your car to an international border crossing between Canada and the United States, or between Mexico and the United States, a long-distance camera scans your license plate. Instantly the U.S. Customs computer database compares your license plate number against the three national motor vehicle registry databases, plus the Customs search-and-seize list and national police and security files of the United States, Canada, and Mexico. When the pleasant Customs and Immigration agent leans out of the booth and asks where you live, where you were born, and who is the registered owner of your vehicle, he or she already knows the answers!

In the five seconds you waited to drive across the red line to approach the Customs agent, the optical scanning system that read your license plate also accessed Immigration, Customs, and State Department records. So the agent knows your vehicle registration, driver's license number, and any records on file with the police. He or she will know if you have outstanding parking tickets and how many trips you've made across the border. The Customs and Immigration computers of the United States and Canada keep records of every time you enter and leave the country. If your answers to the Customs agent's questions are inconsistent with the information displayed on the computer screen, he or she will pull you out of line to undergo a secondary interrogation.

LOSS OF COMPUTER SECURITY

When personal computers were first coming into widespread use, users felt their privacy was protected because they had passwords. Some users didn't even bother to change their passwords regularly.

Today, using a password or PIN (personal identification number) provides virtually no protection against fraud, identity theft, or an outsider's illegally obtaining your personal information. Many passwords are easily guessed through personal knowledge about the user, or the password may be discovered through use of a sophisticated password-cracking software program. Also, spyware programs can be installed on your hard drive when you open a Trojan horse e-mail. Spyware can then monitor every keystroke on your computer, detecting and revealing your passwords. Studies estimate that as many as 90 percent of computers have been penetrated by spyware programs.[2]

In addition to hackers sending out Trojan horse programs via e-mail, your computer use can be tracked by many other interested parties. A variety of people and groups routinely use tracking software to monitor computer activity. This includes parents monitoring their children's Internet activities, suspicious spouses monitoring possibly illicit spousal behavior, employers intrusively monitoring employees' communications and activities, FBI and NSA investigators' monitoring, and criminals seeking to enrich themselves through computer crimes and identity theft.

Corporate security specialists have found that the misuse of computer passwords has seriously compromised the security of many corporations' computers. Employees often choose passwords that are easy to remember, selecting them based on variations of family birthdays, the name of their dog, or even their home address. With access to basic information about an employee, a competent hacker can make educated guesses regarding probable passwords. Additionally, password-search programs are shared by hackers on the Internet. The programs attempt to access computers by trying tens of thousands of password variations. Even more troubling is that people foolishly write down their password and leave it in their wallet or office, where it can easily be discovered.

Using the same password for years without changing it, or giving a password to another employee in an emergency situation and then forgetting to change it afterward, can breach the user's as well as the corporation's security.

BIOMETRIC SECURITY IDENTIFICATION

Although debit and credit cards with either magnetic strips or embedded microchips and passwords have been used to provide identification and access to secure computer systems, companies are increasingly turning to biologically based biometric identification systems to enhance their security. These biometric systems incorporate various elements of your physical makeup to provide an ID system that can't be counterfeited by any other person.

Biometric systems use biological information such as iris scans, fingerprints, hand geometry, and even computerized facial-recognition systems. Numerous bank ATMs have closed-circuit television cameras capable of photographing each customer's iris as he or she stands in front of the ATM. This detailed picture of the iris is compared with the computer database's file of iris patterns for each bank customer. This validates identities without the customer having to memorize a PIN. It is virtually impossible for anyone to counterfeit your unique iris or retina scan, your fingerprints, hand geometry, voiceprint, or your DNA. Intriguingly, while identical twins share identical DNA, they have separate and unique fingerprints.

Until the last few years, biometric ID applications were relatively rare, quite expensive, and not easily implemented in situations where large numbers of people need to be monitored, such as airport security checkpoints and military bases. Fingerprint sensors and voiceprint and signature-recognition systems previously cost an average of a thousand dollars or more. New biometric systems can be obtained for a few hundred dollars each. As a result of significantly lower costs, governments, corporations, and institutions such as hospitals are using these technologies much more widely.

New applications have been developed that are capable of examining high volumes of biometric information at an acceptably low cost. These applications are being used to identify users of computer networks, ATMs, keyless entry systems in office complexes, mobile phones, and other embedded security systems. In high-security offices and manufacturing plants, biometric identification technology may soon supersede the use of passkeys and photo identification badges.

The Rapid Spread of Fingerprint Scanners

NEC Technologies Inc. developed advanced fingerprint-recognition systems, with the majority being used by governments and large corporations. A system called TouchPass permits organizations using Microsoft Windows software and IBM-compatible computers to control access to confidential data by requiring employees to verify their fingerprint ID. Compaq Computer Corporation markets a miniaturized fingerprint scanner at a cost of less than a hundred dollars so that companies can identify authorized personnel and prevent others from gaining access to financial and technical files.

Many military bases, as well as organizations such as banks, are introducing fingerprint scanners to control access to high-security areas. Some hospitals, such as LaPorte Hospital in Indiana, have introduced the HealthID fingerprint-recognition system for hospital staff as well as for patients. The fingerprint scanners ensure that only authorized staff can access patient files. The absolutely reliable identification of every patient will also avoid the risk of inadvertently giving a patient the wrong medication or medical procedure.

Unfortunately, many of the current fingerprint scanners cannot acquire a reliable and readable fingerprint from each person's hand. Existing technology measures the difference in the electrical capacity between the dead skin layer that forms ridges and swirls on your fingertip and the air spaces between the ridges. For example, if a person's skin is very dry due to old age or disease, or if the skin's surface is contaminated due to excessive oil, the system will not be able to read the fingerprint accurately. An engineer working for Harris Corporation in Melbourne, Florida, invented an integrated circuit fingerprint reader, using existing computer technology, called FingerLoc. When a fingertip is placed on the computer chip, the sensors detect the electrical potential from underlying ridges and valleys in the subsurface layer of live skin. This technology provides a much higher level of security because it can read any fingerprint regardless of the individual's skin condition.

ING Direct Canada offers customers a computer mouse that recognizes the fingerprints of an authorized user by comparing them to fingerprints on file in the corporation's database. If an unauthorized person attempts to impersonate the customer and use the mouse, the corporation's security system will detect the attempt and terminate the communication.[3]

The fact that each human has absolutely unique fingerprints that may be used to establish identification has been known since ancient times. Archaeologists in Asia have discovered that early Chinese pottery and ancient Babylonian clay tablets were marked by the artisan by pressing his thumb into the clay before it was fired. The Bible, in the oldest book in Scripture, may actually refer to the fact that God has identified each human with a unique fingerprint: "He sealeth up the hand of every man; that all men may know his work" (Job 37:7).

Facial-Recognition Computer Systems

A significant challenge facing identification systems was the inability of computer software programs to accurately differentiate between the details that compose a photograph of a human face. However, a computer software program has been developed that uses so-called fuzzy logic, which mimics the ability of the human brain to instantly identify facial patterns. Another promising facial-recognition system digitizes a photograph of a human face using 65,536 pixels to create a ten-dimension feature vector. These systems allow the computer to instantaneously compare photos of an individual taken at different times and accurately identify if they are of the same person.

National security, immigration, and police agencies are interested in the possibilities of making greater use of facial-recognition systems. One major application would be to monitor and identify individuals whose images are captured on hidden surveillance cameras at various ports of entry and international airports. These systems would greatly enhance the ability of government authorities to identify and arrest terrorists, drug dealers, covert agents, or international criminals. At the same time, the advanced development and extensive utilization of facial-recognition systems in tandem with closed-circuit television cameras in public places is a significant link in the chain that could produce the global totalitarian police state of the coming Antichrist as described in the book of Revelation.

Detecting Liars and Terrorists

As far back as the 1970s, researchers studied videotape to identify signs that showed a person was lying. When they slowed down the tape, they could determine that a lying person exhibited fleeting but very distinct microexpressions. The almost invisible facial signs lasted less than one-tenth of a second.[4]

Making use of research such as this, the Israeli government launched a sophisticated psychological behavior detection training program for Israeli security officers. The goal was to implement a reliable method to identify potential terrorists at Ben-Gurion Airport and numerous other likely target locations in Israel. Security personnel now watch for signals on airline passengers, such as subtle body language and tiny facial clues revealed for only a fraction of a second. The trained observer might be the El Al airline officer at the ticket desk, a flight attendant, a maintenance man, or the woman who checks your ticket at the gate.

America's Department of Homeland Security and Transportation Security Administration have adopted a similar security and surveillance program. More than a dozen U.S. airports now have up to five hundred behavior detection officers on the job looking for terrorists, illegal immigrants, and persons smuggling contraband. The theory behind this surveillance program is that whenever individuals attempt to conceal their genuine emotions, they invariably reveal those emotions in tiny facial expressions that last a fraction of a second. Microexpressions express real but hidden emotions such as fear, hatred, and disgust— all of which are associated with attempted deception. While the microexpressions are not noticed by ordinary observers, specially trained security officers can detect them.

Also utilized in the effort are surveillance cameras that record passengers' fleeting emotional reactions to questions asked by security officers. Security officers usually work in pairs, with one officer observing a suspicious traveler's activities while a second officer pretends to be focused on other passengers. But in fact the second officer is carefully observing the smallest facial expressions of the person being questioned. Naturally, if the security officers detect signs of continuing deception, they refer the suspicious individual to a much more intense evaluation in a secure room.

U.S. Department of Homeland Security spokesman Jay M. Cohen revealed that American customs officers are automating passenger screening by using video computer surveillance to analyze much more than facial expressions and body language. These surveillance tools measure and analyze heart rate, respiration rate, body temperature, and verbal responses, as well as microexpressions, to detect dangerous passengers.[5]

DNA AND GENETIC TESTING

Each cell in the human body contains deoxyribonucleic acid (DNA), embodying the complete genetic blueprint to build, maintain, and repair every organ and process within a person's body. Your genetic information is absolutely unique. It differs from every other person on earth, with the sole exception being identical twins.

DNA testing has proven to be a phenomenally useful in the criminal justice system. Suspects in criminal investigations are commonly identified, apprehended, and convicted (and occasionally acquitted) based on DNA evidence. Anyone who watches police dramas on television is aware of how DNA can be left behind at and gathered from crime scenes.

It is obvious that the continued accumulation of DNA samples from criminal suspects and convicted prisoners, and from members of the military and law enforcement communities, will ultimately make it possible to identify the majority of suspects in criminal investigations. However, the downside to these developments is, again, an infringement of our privacy. Forensic scientists state that it is virtually impossible to enter a room without leaving some microscopic biological evidence. Your physical presence anywhere will leave behind saliva, blood, flakes of dry skin, sweat, or a strand of hair. Eventually it may be impossible for anyone to escape the police and intelligence agencies of a future totalitarian government.

More than 50 percent of all violent crimes, including rape and murder, are committed by individuals who were arrested previously on suspicion of committing the same type of crime. Since 1994, Congress has mandated that each state collect DNA samples from all violent offenders and all prison inmates. The system requiring that all DNA data must be instantly linked to the national computer database was introduced by the FBI in October 1998. This database, originally called CODIS (Combined DNA Index System) and later changed to the National DNA Index System (NDIS), by early 2009 had archived more than 6,730,749 offender profiles.[6] The NDIS helps the police and courts in every state to instantly compare crime-scene DNA samples to the national database. By June 2007, a similar DNA database in the United Kingdom contained more than four million offender profiles. It has been used to identify in excess of thirty thousand criminals.

The value of DNA evidence is beyond question. A motorcycle police officer in St. Petersburg, Florida, was following a suspect thought to have been involved in a string of robberies and rapes. When the police officer noticed that the suspect spit on the pavement while stopped at a traffic light, the officer stopped his car, took out a paper towel, and gathered the evidence. When the sample was analyzed, the DNA from the saliva matched the DNA sample found on the rape victims. Within a few days the suspect was arrested.[7]

The National Institute of Justice, the research department of the U.S. Department of Justice, has funded research in laboratories around the nation to design devices the size of credit cards capable of analyzing the DNA of biological samples while at crime scenes. The main goal of this research program is to create portable technology for police investigators to immediately identify the DNA of the perpetrator and to instantly compare that DNA sample with those of previous crime suspects from the National DNA Index System.

Another company, Nanogen, developed a portable DNA-analyzing microchip-based device in a plastic cartridge that can be fitted into a briefcase and used with a networked laptop computer. Nanogen's device will interface with the FBI's DNA database and instantly compare DNA samples found at a crime scene with the DNA of an existing criminal profile. The technology involves dissolving the smallest sample of biological evidence (hair, saliva, or skin) in a chemical solution that is then extracted through chemical reactions. The extracted DNA is placed in the plastic cartridge in the briefcase reader, where the short tandem repeats of the DNA sample are analyzed. These repeats produce a unique DNA "fingerprint" that can instantly be compared with the DNA samples of millions of criminals on file with the FBI.[8]

While these remarkable advances assist police officers and other agents of law enforcement, the fight against crime, terrorism, and illegal immigration has seriously diminished our right to privacy. Even when the goals seem legitimate—such as protecting citizens against fraud and identity theft—the result is the same. We are progressively losing our privacy.

PART 2

USING TECHNOLOGY TO RULE THE WORLD

CHAPTER 5

THE GROWING THREAT OF PROJECT ECHELON

If You Think You Still Have Any Privacy, You're Wrong

Every hour of every day the largest intelligence agency on earth, the U.S. National Security Agency (NSA), and its sister intelligence agencies in the United Kingdom, Canada, Australia, and New Zealand are eavesdropping on every one of your communications. Project Echelon records every phone call, fax, and e-mail. It tracks all your Internet surfing.

You might think this sounds too alarmist, or perhaps paranoid, or even like a plot for a high-tech thriller. But this is not fiction, and it's not just my imagination. It's reality. And because of Project Echelon, the last shred of privacy you thought you had is gone.

Why would democratic governments monitor virtually all our daily communications? We will examine that later in this chapter, but first we will look at the evidence of the existence and the goals of Project Echelon. Because of this all-invasive technology network, you can no longer take for granted your privacy and freedom.

When I first began this research in the 1990s, most people had never heard of Project Echelon. Those who were aware of it believed it never would be turned against personal communications and business activities of the citizens of democratic nations. They preferred to believe this massive intelligence-gathering network would be limited to protecting the West against potential enemies in Russia, China, Iran, and certain Arab nations.

AN INTRODUCTION TO PROJECT ECHELON

The largest intelligence-gathering facility within Echelon is located on the moors of North Yorkshire at a U.S. military base at Menwith Hill, United Kingdom. One longtime observer described it by saying, "The UK base...has its own independent electrical power station to ensure uninterrupted operations. Menwith Hill is probably the largest espionage station on the planet. Approximately two-thirds of its staff is American intelligence agents.... Thirty huge satellite reception radomes, code-named Moonpenny, looking like giant golf balls, sit somewhat conspicuously among the large flocks of English sheep within the security fences of the well-guarded base."[1]

The radomes contain collection dishes that gather the billions of daily radio signals intercepted from 120 Echelon geostationary satellites orbiting the earth. This is in addition to the massive number of intercepted messages flowing through huge undersea cables that carry the majority of the transatlantic and transpacific Internet and e-mail communications. In addition to recording and analyzing English-language communications, Echelon computers capture and translate conversations in more than seventy other languages in a continual search for terrorist and enemy-nation intelligence communications. Every day the Echelon system monitors millions of messages. The world's most sophisticated computers are hunting for clues to plans for terrorist attacks and other threats against the West.

Menwith Hill's station uses a multitude of secret electronic interception systems—including the Vortex, Magnum, and Orion spy satellite systems—to collect data from the supposedly secret communications of many nations and corporations. It monitors all communications from the European Union states, Russia, and the rest of Asia. Echelon collects virtually all electronic communications from European governments, corporations, and private individuals and intercepts all transatlantic communications to and from North America. Menwith Hill is under the control of the NSA, in cooperation with British intelligence, which shares the vast intelligence spoils.

This remarkable spy station was built on property that carries the three main digital fiberoptic cables from Europe through the United Kingdom to America, each of which is simultaneously transmitting up to a hundred thousand calls. These vital communications cables go directly through the Menwith Hill building to enable the Echelon computers to download every communication without delaying any of the calls.

Echelon uses a vast array of collection platforms. In addition to NSA satellites circling high above the globe, high-altitude military and NSA aircraft, naval vessels, a large fleet of mobile surveillance vans, and the tapping of undersea fiberoptic cables, Echelon uses numerous secret interception technologies that penetrate mobile or desktop computers as well as virtually all phone and radio communications.[2]

The terrorist attacks on the World Trade Center and the Pentagon on September 11, 2001, forced the United States and its Western allies to adopt an entirely new kind of counterterrorist warfare. New terror threats called for strategies and tactics to enable Western intelligence agencies to gather vast amounts of communication and financial data. The aim is to identify and destroy radical Islamic terror cells throughout the world. Tracking the movement of finances, weapons purchases, and other financial transactions is a vital part of the global struggle against terrorism.

However, Echelon is a double-edged sword. It provides a massive amount of vital intelligence about the communications, plans, targets, and members of the most dedicated enemies of Western civilization. However, it also gathers and possesses a staggering amount of detailed information regarding the billions of daily communications of ordinary citizens and corporations. This intrusion into the affairs of private citizens and businesses poses a very real threat to our freedom.

Since 9/11, there has been widespread agreement that the threat from Islamic terrorists requires democratic governments to use every available technology to monitor terrorist communications. However, this intelligence gathering could easily become the means of creating the most effective totalitarian state ever conceived. Few in the West doubt the seriousness of the threat posed by spies and radical Islam. However, will combating these threats also rob every one of us of our cherished freedom?

THE BACKGROUND OF PROJECT ECHELON

In the twentieth century the United States and other Western democracies were faced with the rise of powerful dictators and both fascist and communist totalitarian governments in many parts of the world. Growing threats to national security demonstrated the need for the best intelligence capabilities to protect the West against tyrants such as Adolf Hitler, Joseph Stalin, and later Mao Zedong.

Echelon was launched by the NSA following World War II. The global spy system was a top-secret Anglo-American project designed to intercept and analyze virtually every message that was transmitted by any means.

Echelon is managed by five Western nations: the United States, the United Kingdom, Canada, Australia, and New Zealand. In 1948 these five countries entered into a secret agreement called UKUSA to spy on Russia and its Warsaw Pact allies during the cold war.[3]

The NSA handles communications coming out of Russia east of the Ural Mountains and most of North and South America. Australia's facility covers Southeast Asia, including India and Indonesia, and the South Pacific islands. Israel is a key allied associate and provides detailed intelligence of secret military and terrorist activities within the Arab nations and Russia. Israel's secret electronic surveillance facility is called Unit 8200 and is located in the northern suburbs of Tel Aviv, known as Herzliya. Unit 8200 accumulates and analyzes the intelligence collected by a large number of interception satellite receiver stations throughout Israel, including Mount Hermon in the northern Golan Heights, Nahariyah on the border with Lebanon, Mitzpah Ramon in the southern Negev Desert, and a remote southern site on Dahlak Island in the Red Sea. The United Kingdom covers Eastern Europe and Russia, while New Zealand covers the Pacific nations.

The member nations cooperate in such a way that none of them is spying on the communications of citizens, businesses, and officials from its own nation. By monitoring the private communications of other member nations, they avoid legal prohibitions against a democratic government's spying on communications of its own citizens. This transparent violation of the law enables each country to technically deny that it illegally intercepts the electronic communications of its own citizens.

Mike Frost, a former member of Canada's Communications Security Establishment, told the Canadian press that the five cooperating nations of Echelon agree to spy on the others' citizens and then send the data to the appropriate intelligence agency using encrypted computer transmissions. Frost wrote the book *Spyworld* to detail his past spying activities. He stated, "They circumvent their own legislation by asking the other countries to do it for them. We do it for them, they do it for us and then they can stand up in the House [of Commons] and say we do not target the communications of Canadian citizens."[4]

Echelon's global electronic eavesdropping covers virtually every telephone call, fax transmission, and e-mail message. The intercepted communications are compiled and analyzed by banks of NSA supercomputers at Fort Meade, Maryland. The billions of intercepted communications are searched for keywords identified by the five-member intelligence agencies in Echelon dictionaries. This worldwide intelligence vacuum cleaner is constantly sifting through billions of simultaneous phone calls and e-mail messages in search of any use of thousands of keywords, key telephone numbers, passwords, and voiceprints of targeted individuals, whether terrorists, spies, or criminals.

While most of the West's other surveillance systems are focused on enemy nations' military developments, plans, weapons, and capabilities, Echelon is unique in that its primary espionage focus involves nonmilitary civilian targets.

HOW ECHELON DOES ITS WORK

Project Echelon uses the most advanced spy satellites, illegal wiretaps, and the fastest supercomputers to analyze and record billions of global communications annually. Targets include all local, cellular, and long distance phone calls, fax and telex transmissions, Internet communications—including Web surfing, newsgroups, chat rooms, and e-mail—and all global radio traffic. The Echelon system design involves the careful positioning of communications interception stations throughout the world to collect downlinked satellite, microwave, cellular, and ground-based fiberoptic communications traffic. Echelon intercepts data from the series of twenty international telecommunications satellites (Intelsats) that circle the globe above the equator.[5]

The surveillance system has three separate but essential functions: interception, analysis, and reporting. The interception function includes a global communications monitoring system. The analysis function of Echelon is completed at NSA headquarters at Fort Meade, Maryland, by enormous numbers of supercomputers and thousands of intelligence analysts. The reporting function involves a system of daily information passed to the various intelligence agencies and the leaders of the Western nations.

Echelon communications intercepts are processed using NSA's computer analysis, including voice recognition, translations from more than seventy languages, artificial intelligence neural networks, and optical character recognition (OCR) programs. The computer programs search for keywords and phrases listed by each of the five member nations' intelligence agencies. Intercepted communications are recorded and transcribed for future analysis. At Echelon's Menwith Hill site in Britain, a sophisticated voice-recognition program called Voicecast can identify and target any individual voice pattern among six billion humans throughout the globe. (Each voice is as unique as a person's fingerprints, DNA, or iris scan.) This means that every subsequent telephone call involving that person's voice can be captured and transcribed by the agency for future analysis. Useful information is forwarded to the national intelligence agency that originally requested the intercept. The vast majority of Echelon intercepts are innocent messages that contain no key names, words, addresses, or phone numbers. The millions of useless messages are erased by Echelon computers and are never analyzed by a human operator.[6]

The governments' justification for maintaining Echelon's universal surveillance program is that Western society must be protected against the so-called Four Horsemen of the Infocalypse: terrorists, drug dealers, sexual predators, and organized crime.[7] However, the phenomenally intrusive surveillance technologies could easily be used by government authorities in the future as a tool of totalitarian police control against ordinary citizens. Simon Davies, director of Privacy International and fellow at the London School of Economics, warned, "History demonstrates that information in the hands of Authority will inevitably be used for unintended and often malevolent purposes."[8]

Keywords from the Echelon Dictionary

An abbreviated list of keywords used by Echelon to search for possibly relevant material is given below. This list, which was provided by several individuals in the intelligence community, gives examples of the topics an intelligence agency may consider worthy of a follow-up investigation. The real list of keywords from the Echelon Dictionary Oratory program would involve many thousands of possibilities, constantly updated by each of the five allied agencies.

Explosives, guns, assassination, conspiracy, primers, detonators, nuclear, ambush, IRS, BATF, hostages, munitions, weapons, TNT, presidential motorcade, grenades, rockets, fuses, mortars, incendiary device, security forces, infiltration, assault team, evasion, detection, mission, body armor, timing devices, booby traps, silencers, Uzi, AK-47, napalm, Air Force One, special forces, terrorism, National Information Infrastructure, hackers, encryption, espionage, FBI, Secret Service, White House, Infowar, FINCEN, RCMP, GRU, SAS, Echelon, Spetznaz, Psyops, TELINT, Bletchley Park, clandestine, NSO, security, sniper, Electronic Surveillance, al Qaeda, Muslim Brotherhood, Islamic Jihad, counterterrorism, interception, Gamma, keyhole, SEAL Merlin, white noise, top secret,

TRW, counterintelligence, industrial espionage, Minox, Rand Corporation, Wackenhutt, Scud, SecDef, SWAT, Fort Meade, NORAD, Delta Force, SEAL, Black-Ops, Area 51, TEMPEST, Pine Gap, Menwith, Sayeret Mat'Kal, Sayeret Golani, Delta, GRU, GSS, Crypto AG.[9]

Within seconds of a phone call being made anywhere in the world, a suspected or confirmed terrorist, organized crime figure, or spy can be identified by Echelon based on his or her voiceprint. The caller can be quickly identified and the call terminated. The FBI and NSA can override the signal from the suspect's phone and keep the connection open even after the suspect hangs up. They can then use a simulated computer voice impersonating the suspect on the substituted call. The call can be redirected using the simulated voice to create chaos within the terror group or criminal organization. When a suspect caller is identified, his or her location can be determined within thirty yards. Don't believe what you see in action movies, where the criminal hangs up the phone in less than thirty seconds and thereby foils the ability of the FBI or NSA to trace his call. New intercept technology needs only seconds to determine a caller's phone number and location.[10]

DOES ECHELON REALLY EXIST?

At this point you might be wondering if such a draconian surveillance system really is possible. And if it is, would our government actually use it to spy on its own citizens?

In public statements both U.S. and British officials continue to deny that Project Echelon exists. In April 1999 the American Civil Liberties Union contacted members of Congress about the dangers of Echelon. When the official NSA spokeswoman was asked about the existence of Echelon, she replied, "We don't confirm or deny the existence of Echelon."[11]

After decades of U.S. government denials of Echelon, overwhelming documentation now exists to prove that the shadowy surveillance system does indeed exist. An article in the *Guardian* declared, "For years it has been the subject of bitter controversy, its existence repeatedly claimed but never officially acknowledged. At last, the leaked draft of a report…by the European parliament removes any lingering doubt: Echelon, a shadowy, US-led worldwide electronic spying network, is a reality."[12]

And as far back as December 19, 1999, BBC News reported that Australian intelligence officials admitted that the Echelon system does actually exist. Bill Blick, Australia's inspector general of intelligence and security, confirmed to the BBC that Australia's Defence Signals Directorate (DSD) is that country's component of the five-nation Echelon network. "As you would expect there are a large amount of radio communications floating around in the atmosphere, and agencies such as DSD collect those communications in the interests of their national security," Blick stated. Further, he admitted that the intercepted communications are shared with allies such as Britain, Canada, New Zealand, and the United States.[13]

Journalist Nicky Hager conducted interviews with agents and technicians working with New Zealand's General Communications Security Bureau (GCSB). They described a vast network of Echelon communication interception stations throughout the world.[14] And in 1991 a retired British intelligence officer who had worked for Echelon spoke anonymously in a documentary to the UK producers of Granada Television's *World in Action*. The officer confirmed the existence of the worldwide surveillance program. He admitted that all the data was passed through an analysis computer program called Dictionary, which examined billions of messages weekly for any messages of interest.

Mike Frost, a former Canadian operative, explained how the intelligence agencies' "embassy collection" operations used their nations' embassy buildings in various foreign capitals to act as interception stations for Echelon. Embassy buildings are ideal intelligence collection sites because they are usually situated near the target government's major ministries, normally at the center of the target nation's microwave communications networks. Frost claimed that after secretly transporting sophisticated satellite receivers and processors inside diplomatic pouches into their own embassy, NSA spies would set up their radio and microwave reception dishes on the roofs of the embassy, often disguised as air conditioning and heating pipes.[15]

POTENTIAL ABUSE OF INTELLIGENCE GATHERING

Echelon was built during the cold war, when the spread of nuclear weapons forced both East and West to face the prospect of a nuclear Armageddon. Today the threat of attack has multiplied, with terror groups and rogue nations greatly expanding the list of enemies. As the cost to produce biological, chemical, and atomic "dirty bomb" weapons continues to drop, the number of terrorist groups—radical Islamic and others—is rising. While I hate the thought of intelligence agencies monitoring all our private and corporate communications, I am forced to admit that Western governments need to do all they can to guard against the growing threat of terrorist attacks. It is essential that our intelligence agencies use the best communications interception equipment available to detect plans for enemy attacks.

Yet history records that almost every technological advance has been abused by political, military, and police authorities. The first use of technology by authority tends to be in the area of communications control, security, and policing. However, history also reveals that almost every new technology is eventually used by ordinary citizens for free and private communication and political freedom.

One example is the introduction of the printing press in Europe in the mid-1400s. Initially it was monopolized under exclusive license by the political authorities of that day. However, citizens were soon using presses to print political pamphlets and Bibles. Bibles were immediately translated from the original languages into English, French, and German to enable Christians to read the Word of God in their own languages for the first time in a thousand years. This facilitated the Protestant Reformation, the Enlightenment, and the greatest advance in political liberty and religious freedom in history. Likewise, advances in computer technology and the Internet present both enormous opportunities and terrible dangers to our political and religious freedoms.

The lesson of history, as declared by England's Lord Acton more than a century ago, is that "power tends to corrupt; absolute power corrupts absolutely." A balanced historical appraisal of the growth of political, military, and social control shows that we have reached a truly unprecedented time. No leader in the past has ever held such potential political and police power as the Echelon system provides to the intelligence and security agencies of the governments of the West. With the major Western powers examining every electronic communication, we need to realize that our liberty and freedom stand in the greatest jeopardy of all time.

The record shows a pattern in which intelligence, defense, and law enforcement agencies find ways to evade the legal constraints enacted by the U.S. Congress or Canadian Parliament to protect our privacy and civil liberties. Following the end of the cold war, military defense groups and intelligence agencies sought new missions to justify their budgets. Often surveillance technologies are shifted to civilian applications and away from their former role in national defense against enemy nations.

Christopher Simpson, who has written four books on national security issues, described the sheer volume of data that is collected from the private communications of ordinary citizens each month:

> We're talking tens of millions of volumes if it was printed out on
> pages.... As we move into this interconnected electronic world, you've
> got Big Brothers, and you've got Little Brothers.... Little Brothers are
> companies like supermarkets and Internet companies that keep an eye
> on you. And you've got Big Brother that keeps an eye on you. The
> Biggest Brother of all is the Echelon system.[16]

The U.S. National Security Council proposed in July 1998 that American intelligence agencies should constantly monitor the computer networks of banks, telecommunications corporations, transportation companies, and non-military government operations in an attempt to protect vital communications data networks. Only one month later the Justice Department proposed legislation to grant the FBI the legal authority to place encryption-breaking devices and secret surveillance software programs in citizens' computers, in their homes and in their offices, during criminal investigations.[17]

WHO IS WATCHING THE WATCHERS?

The Echelon system has known all about you for many years. Now you know something about Echelon. The only hope for this surveillance technology remaining a servant of democratic government and its citizens and not becoming a dictatorial master is to ensure there is a system of continual, powerful presidential and congressional oversight to watch the watchers. It is my hope that the growing revelations from media around the world about the capabilities and dangers associated with the vital and powerful Project Echelon will encourage our government's representatives to demand democratic accountability of these necessary but also inherently dangerous surveillance technologies.

More than three quarters of a century ago, Louis Brandeis, a well-respected Supreme Court justice, warned against the danger to our freedom from the increasing capabilities of the government to monitor the communications and private lives of average citizens. In 1928, during a case involving police wiretapping, Brandeis wrote a profound dissenting opinion describing the fundamental right of each citizen to privacy in his thoughts and private papers. He wrote against the government's abuse of the citizen's Fifth Amendment right—that of not being forced to give testimony or evidence against oneself—as well as the Fourth Amendment prohibition against illegal search and seizure.

When the Fourth and Fifth Amendments were adopted, "the form that evil had theretofore taken" had been necessarily simple. Force and violence were then the only means known to man by which a government could directly effect self-incrimination. It could compel the individual to testify—a compulsion effected, if need be, by torture. It could secure possession of his papers and other articles incident to his private life—a seizure effected, if need be, by breaking and entry. Protection against such invasion of "the sanctities of a man's home and the privacies of life" was provided in the Fourth and Fifth Amendments by specific language. *Boyd v. United States,* 116 U.S. 616, 630, 6 S.Ct. 524, 29 L.Ed. 746. But "time works changes, brings into existence new conditions and purposes." Subtler and more far-reaching means of invading privacy have become available to the government. Discovery and invention have made it possible for the government, by means far more effective than stretching upon the rack, to obtain disclosure in court of what is whispered in the closet.

Moreover, "in the application of a Constitution, our contemplation cannot be only of what has been, but of what may be." The progress of science in furnishing the government with means of espionage is not likely to stop with wire tapping. Ways may some day be developed by which the government, without removing papers from secret drawers, can reproduce them in court, and by which it will be enabled to expose to a jury the most intimate occurrences of the home. Advances in the psychic and related sciences may bring means of exploring unexpressed beliefs, thoughts and emotions. "That places the liberty of every man in the hands of every petty officer" was said by James Otis of much lesser intrusions than these. To Lord Camden a far slighter intrusion seemed "subversive of all the comforts of society." Can it be that the Constitution affords no protection against such invasions of individual security?[18]

Brandeis expressed well-founded concerns about the potential dangers to our constitutional rights posed by the government's invasion of an individual's privacy. Brandeis would be astonished to know that all democratic governments routinely perform around-the-clock surveillance and record the data in massive databases. Every citizen is monitored, based on the slim chance that he or she may now, or at some point in the future, become a legitimate target of the police or a national intelligence agency. Brandeis also warned us to be most on guard against the growing threats to our freedom and privacy when government authorities attempt to justify their intrusive surveillance activities for seemingly beneficial reasons:

> Experience should teach us to be most on our guard to protect liberty when the government's purposes are beneficent. Men born to freedom are naturally alert to repel invasion of their liberty by evil-minded rulers. The greatest dangers to liberty lurk in insidious encroachment by men of zeal, well-meaning but without understanding.[19]

In the past, students of the Bible's prophecies have wondered how John's prediction in the book of Revelation regarding the Antichrist's global monitoring of all citizens could ever be fulfilled literally. Until the last decade it was impossible for any government, even Nazi Germany or communist Russia and China, to provide continuous monitoring of every citizen, no matter how many informers or secret police agents were employed. But today, citizens of Western democracies are under closer surveillance than anyone who lived in Nazi Germany or the Soviet Union.

The development of the Echelon surveillance system and the parallel systems used by Russia, China, and the European Union show very clearly how it will be possible for a future world dictator, the Antichrist, to exercise total surveillance and control over the world's population. The only hope for continued freedom and liberty will be found in the certain promise of the Word of God that Jesus Christ will return as prophesied to liberate humanity from the satanic oppression of the Antichrist.

CHAPTER 6

NEW WEAPONS IN THE ARSENAL OF THE NEW WORLD ORDER

"Mass Destruction" Doesn't Even Begin to Tell the Story

In the near future, warring nations will go into battle with weapons that seem to come out of science fiction. Weapons of astonishing power, as well as weapons that can selectively kill predetermined victims, will transform global warfare. At the same time, remarkable advances in surveillance technology as well as nonlethal weapons provide police forces and intelligence agencies with overwhelming power to monitor and control citizens in their own countries.

When we examine these ominous developments in light of the prophetic warnings of Scripture, it is clear that we are witnessing the beginning of the events that will culminate in the rise of the Antichrist. These new tools of war will be used by his totalitarian government, and they will appear in the final battle of this age—the battle of Armageddon.

WEAPONS OF THE COMING GLOBAL GOVERNMENT

Men's hearts failing them for fear,...for the powers of heaven shall be shaken.—Jesus, in Luke 21:26

The biblical prophets saw, thousands of years ago, the incredible force and lethal power of weapons of war in the end times. For example, Jesus' quote in Luke 21 clearly could refer to the then-unheard-of use of nuclear weapons in the last days.

Likewise, the prophet John may have referred to the use of nuclear weapons: "And the heaven departed as a scroll when it is rolled together; and every mountain and island were moved out of their places" (Revelation 6:14). Using the descriptive language available to him, John depicts what appears to be a devastating thermonuclear blast that destroys mountains and islands in a way that, in human terms, could be accomplished only by nuclear weapons.

The Old Testament prophet Zechariah appears to have referred to neutron bombs in his prophecy regarding the city of Jerusalem at the end of the battle of Armageddon. "And this shall be the plague wherewith the LORD will smite all the people that have fought against Jerusalem; Their flesh shall consume away while they stand upon their feet, and their eyes shall consume away in their holes, and their tongue shall consume away in their mouth" (Zechariah 14:12). The prophet's description that "the flesh shall consume away" describes the terrible effect of neutron bombs, which use gamma rays that destroy the flesh of their victims without vaporizing bones, buildings, or equipment. Only the victim's skeleton remains, and nearby buildings and equipment are undamaged.

Isaiah appears to have foreseen the development of airplanes. He prophesied about God defending Jerusalem in the last days' generation. The prophet described methods of defense with the phrases "as birds flying" and "passing over he will preserve it." Isaiah wrote centuries before the birth of Christ, "As birds flying, so will the LORD of hosts defend Jerusalem; defending also he will deliver it; and passing over he will preserve it" (Isaiah 31:5).

This prophecy was fulfilled in 1917. In December of that year, as the Allied Expeditionary Force approached the Turkish army that controlled Jerusalem, Lord Edmund Allenby ordered his small air force to fly over the Holy City. Pilots dropped pamphlets that warned Turkish soldiers to flee the city. Fortunately, rather than fight it out street by street, the Turkish troops fled Jerusalem without firing a shot. Truly, God had defended His Holy City and preserved it through the unprecedented use of Allied planes.

It is difficult to read prophecies of the terrible final worldwide conflict between the allied nations of the East and West during the last days without thinking about the recent development of long-range ballistic missiles with nuclear warheads. John wrote, "And there fell a great star from heaven, burning as it were a lamp, and it fell upon the third part of the rivers, and upon the fountains of waters" (Revelation 8:10). This may be John's description of an incoming missile. Joel may also have described the use of a missile-based weapon: "A fire devoureth before them; and behind them a flame burneth" (Joel 2:3).

Having never seen an armored vehicle, John prophetically described what in his vision appears to be the future use of tanks in the wars of the Tribulation period. "And thus I saw the horses in the vision, and them that sat on them, having breastplates of fire, and of jacinth, and brimstone: and the heads of the horses were as the heads of lions; and out of their mouths issued fire and smoke and brimstone. By these three was the third part of men killed, by the fire, and by the smoke, and by the brimstone, which issued out of their mouths" (Revelation 9:17–18). Modern tanks deliver high-explosive shells, their barrels can act as flamethrowers, and new U.S. tanks can deliver electromagnetic-pulse weapons capable of unbelievable destruction.

Star Trek–Type Phaser Weapons

Since the mid-1960s, Starfleet captains have been issuing the command, "Set phasers to stun." Now HSV Technologies Inc. of Port Orchard, Washington, has developed a nonlethal weapon that creates ultraviolet laser beams that can be aimed from a distance and used against a human or animal. The beams ionize two parallel paths through the air to send an electrical charge that immobilizes the victim. The UV radiation closely replicates the neuroelectric impulses that control skeletal muscles. The beam overrides the normal repetition rate of such impulses, resulting in uncontrollable muscle contractions. Fortunately, the frequency of the radiation causes no harm to the target's eyes, nor does it adversely affect the heart or diaphragm muscles. Think of this new long-distance weapon as a Taser without wires.

A variation of this technology can be used by a police officer to stop a suspect escaping in a vehicle. The ionized beam instantly disables the ignition system of the target vehicle.[1] Likewise, a customs agent can use the weapon to intermittently disable the engine of a plane carrying contraband, forcing the suspect pilot to land or be forced into a crash landing.

Electrical-Pulse Weapons

Another nonlethal weapon stores in a battery a massive electrical charge that can be released whenever a targeted vehicle drives over a wire laid across a road. Immediately, the huge electrical charge overwhelms the vehicle's ignition, and the vehicle is disabled. A variation of this technology would enable police or the military to send stored electrical power to a targeted building, shorting out computers, lights, and security systems. Other devices send a wave of focused microwave power to a targeted aircraft, railway car, or vehicle to disable its electrical and ignition systems.

The U.S. Air Force Scientific Advisory Board issued a report on the development of electromagnetic weapons that can be pulsed or focused to inhibit a person's muscle function, cause sleepiness, or affect emotions. The federal government's plan to use nonlethal pulsed, electromagnetic, and radio-frequency systems for domestic law enforcement purposes raises serious concern about potential dangers to average citizens. The Air Force Scientific Advisory Board report reveals that nonlethal weapons are designed for use against both domestic and foreign enemies of the U.S. government. The board warned that it is important for the public to understand that just as lethal weapons do not kill the enemy 100 percent of the time, neither will nonlethal weapons always avoid inflicting lethal injuries.

An article published in *Parameters: U.S. Army War College Quarterly* reported on research in Moscow aimed at developing a computer virus named Russian Virus 666. The virus is designed to introduce a subliminal and intermittent pulse pattern on a computer screen that can force a computer operator into a trancelike state. There are several reports that this computer virus program can also induce a subconscious reaction causing changes in a person's perceptions or even a heart arrhythmia.[2]

Photon Directed-Energy Weapons

In *Star Trek* the starship *Enterprise* often goes into battle against an enemy spaceship. In addition to its phasers, the *Enterprise* fires photon torpedoes, "balls" of light energy, across the vacuum of space. The idea that pulses of light energy could be focused and fired effectively at an enemy vessel in space seems implausible to most of us. A major reason to question such a weapon is the tendency of acoustical or electromagnetic energy to disperse as it travels through space.

However, American researchers have developed long-distance directed-energy-beam weapons. Here is the description from a patent issued for the invention: "The invention relates generally to transmission of pulses of energy, and more particularly to the propagation of localized pulses of electromagnetic or acoustic energy over long distances without divergence."[3] The patent issued for this technology describes the effect of the beamed energy as "electromagnetic missiles or bullets" capable of destroying virtually any targeted object at extreme distances.

The "Voice of God" Weapon

The U.S. military also has created a weapon that can project a verbal or even a visual message into the mind of an enemy combatant. Knowledgeable insiders suggest that the designated target actually perceives the message as coming from God (or Allah). Picture a suicide bomber or other terrorist on a mission suddenly hearing a voice in his or her head.

Two technology companies, Holosonic Research Labs and American Technology Corporation, have developed their own versions of sound-directing technology. There are reports that U.S. troops in Iraq and Afghanistan have used a similar system to confuse and disorientate enemy combatants. Some reports suggest that the visualization technology could be adapted to fit the religious expectations of the targeted individual in order to enhance the psychological impact.[4]

A Horrifying Particle-Beam Weapon

During the worst days of street fighting against insurgents in Baghdad in 2004, the U.S. military unleashed a frightening weapon that destroyed enemy targets in an unprecedented way. It can be seen in the film *Star Wars in Iraq* by filmmaker Patrick Dillon. An Iraqi soldier who had fought in three wars, Majid al-Ghazali, described the tank-based particle-beam weapon as being similar to a flamethrower but tremendously more destructive. This weapon shot its target with what appeared to be focused lightning bolts instead of flames of ordinary fire. (View Dillon's *Star Wars in Iraq* at http://star.wars.in.iraq.vaizdelis.lt/.)

During a street battle in his Baghdad neighborhood, al-Ghazali observed the weapon emit a blinding stream of fire and lightning bolts. The tank targeted a bus and three automobiles filled with Iraqi insurgents. The bus melted into a shrinking mass of molten metal approximately the size of a Volkswagen Beetle. Al-Ghazali added that he observed the bodies of hundreds of insurgents around the melted vehicles, but their bodies had shriveled to less than eighteen inches in length.

By the end of that extended street battle, the bodies of at least five hundred insurgents were found to have been instantaneously cooked by this horrifying weapon. Within hours, military bulldozers and work crews buried the melted vehicles and the bodies to prevent further observation. Dillon, a Vietnam-era medic and later a photographer in numerous war zones, was taken to the battleground a few days later by al-Ghazali to view what evidence remained. To Dillon's amazement, they found ample indications of the use of this terrifying weapon, including irregular puddles of melted metal and mounds of fibrous matter that appeared to have originally been the vehicles' tires. Knowledgeable sources suggest that, based on the effect of this weapon, the United States must have employed a devastating electromagnetic or microwave pulse weapon.

Dillon, who in the past had witnessed the devastation caused by flamethrowers, napalm, and white phosphorous, stated in his film that he knew of no previous weapon that might cause a bus to be reduced to a lump of twisted molten metal and instantaneously boil a body down to the size of a baby. He concluded, "God pity humanity if that thing is a preview of what's in store for the 21st century."[5]

An Electronic Gun

Metal Storm is the name of a revolutionary group of weapons created by inventor Mike O'Dwyer. The first Metal Storm weapon is a pod of thirty-six nine-millimeter barrels containing fifteen bullets each. Using an electronic trigger instead of moving mechanical parts to fire the bullets only tiny fractions of a second apart, the weapon delivers an astonishingly deadly blast of more than 500 rounds *in about three-hundredths of a second.* O'Dwyer believes the major application of this devastating weapon is its ability to fire a blizzard of deadly munitions from a ship, creating a defensive shield against incoming missiles.[6]

In comparison, the fastest rate of fire from a conventional shipboard weapon is 10,000 rounds per minute (166 rounds per second), and when bullets leave the conventional weapon, they are approximately one hundred feet apart. In contrast, the bullets fired from Metal Storm approach the target only a half inch apart. The weapon can be adapted to a perimeter defense of troops in the field by firing massive bursts of forty-millimeter grenades to stop incoming mortars or rockets.[7]

A Thermobaric Rifle

After years of research aimed at increasing the power of handheld weapons available to infantrymen, the Department of Defense has equipped soldiers in Iraq and Afghanistan with a thirty-three-inch long weapon that vastly increases their firepower. According to an article in *Wired* magazine, the thermobaric bomb is "a fearsome explosive that sets fire to the air above its target, then sucks the oxygen out of anyone unfortunate enough to have lived through the initial blast." Thermobaric ammunition contains a computer chip that the soldier can program so the charge explodes precisely over the heads of enemy soldiers or terrorists hiding in buildings.[8]

A much larger variant, the Bunker Defeat rocket launcher, is used by soldiers fighting against al Qaeda and Taliban terrorists hiding in large complexes of caves and vast caverns in Afghanistan. When exploded in a cave or building, it injects a flammable mist into the air that creates a fireball when exposed to oxygen. Even if terrorists escape the initial firestorm, a second later the remaining mist sucks all the oxygen out of the cave or building, asphyxiating them. The unique characteristics of thermobaric bombs make them ideal for fighting multiple terrorists occupying multiple areas within a targeted cave or building.[9]

An interesting sidelight is that the September 21, 2008, al Qaeda attack on the Islamabad Marriott Hotel in Pakistan, which left a large hole in front of the hotel, was actually a crude version of a thermobaric bomb. The one-ton truck bomb consisted of improvised explosives including grenades, artillery shells, and a significant amount of aluminum powder that accelerated the bomb's explosive power.[10]

The Silent Guardian Microwave Weapon

A weapon developed by Raytheon, known as the Silent Guardian, is a device the size of a large television plasma screen and is mounted on the back of a Humvee. When energized, the Silent Guardian emits microwaves at a precise frequency that produce unendurable pain by stimulating a targeted person's nerve endings. This can be done over a distance up to a half mile. The device produces a beam that penetrates the skin of the targeted individual only to a depth of one-sixty-fourth of an inch, so the Silent Guardian can't cause visible or permanent injury to the target. Soldiers who volunteered to test the effect of the weapon could not resist fleeing the target area, due to the intense discomfort caused by the microwaves, after only one second.[11]

Similarly, devastating sound waves can be launched by an acoustic cannon. The sound waves disrupt the hearing and other body functions of enemy soldiers in a target zone. Launched from a low-flying helicopter, a narrow beam of low-frequency sound intersects with a separate sound-wave beam originating from another aircraft, creating unendurable bodily discomfort.[12]

A third type of weapon involves a radio frequency that can affect a human target even through a concrete wall. One variation of this weapon focuses a radio frequency at a target, causing his body temperature to rise as high as 107 degrees within seconds. The combatant immediately becomes sick and disoriented and, therefore, disabled.[13]

Speed-of-Light Particle-Beam Weapons

A devastating weapon system developed in military laboratories in the United States, United Kingdom, Russia, China, and Israel falls under the category of directed-energy warfare. This includes military applications of lasers, particle-beam weapons, and microwave weapons used against targets on land, on sea, in air, and in space. Retired Maj. Gen. George J. Keegan Jr., chief of intelligence for the U.S. Air Force, described a beam weapon known as a collective accelerator. It uses powerful magnets to accelerate the orbits of electrons around the nuclei of atoms to the speed of light. It then pulses the resulting stream of protons hundreds of times per second. The pulse of protons carries an electrical charge of tens of billions of electron-volts, which causes a target to virtually disintegrate.[14]

Radio-Frequency Weapons

A number of research projects have reported the development of weapons using radio frequencies to produce large amounts of static electrical energy capable of destroying targets such as computers. A new form of these weapons, transient electromagnetic devices (TEDs), could be used to debilitate the electronic infrastructure of societies, including government offices, financial institutions, aircraft, medical facilities, and critical electronic equipment of all kinds. These devices can be assembled using widely available electronic parts costing less than five hundred dollars. Electronic frequency weapons generate wide-band radio pulses in the nanosecond and picosecond range, using megawatt power and gigahertz (microwave) frequencies. Directional radio-frequency antennas send radio pulses to attack specific targets. These RF (radio frequency) terrorist weapons could be easily disguised as small satellite dishes.[15] It is possible to protect vital computer systems against RF attacks, but the cost is prohibitive except for the most vital government computer systems.

WEATHER WARFARE

Climate scientists and advanced weapons labs discovered more than three decades ago how to create rain or cause a drought to affect a distant nation. One significant piece of evidence that verifies the development of weather warfare is that the United Nations negotiated a weather modification treaty. The international treaty committed every nation on earth to prohibit the development of weather-control weapons. The agreement was approved by the General Assembly on December 10, 1976.[16]

The military advantage of being able to control the weather over your own nation or that of your enemy has been obvious to generals for decades. In the late 1990s a U.S. Air Force study titled "Weather as a Force Multiplier" described two methods that could be used by approximately the year 2025 to control global weather patterns. One method is to use ionospheric heaters to influence the upper level of the atmosphere. The second is to create clouds "generated by chemical condensation trails (contrails)" that would be released from huge airplane tankers.

U.S. Navy and Air Force researchers at a top-secret base in Gakona, Alaska, developed an ionospheric heater as part of the High-Frequency Active Auroral Research Project (HAARP). HAARP sent tightly focused rays of intense radio-frequency energy into the atmosphere for several years at a time.[17]

The inventor of HAARP, Bernard Eastlund, acknowledged NATO's interest in modifying weather patterns to influence enemy nations. For example, a 1990 NATO report titled "Modification of Tropospheric Propagation Conditions" outlined how the military might use high-altitude tanker planes to spray chemical polymers to modify the atmosphere. The polymers would allow the atmosphere to absorb more electromagnetic radiation, thereby heating the air. According to the report, it is possible to use HAARP to achieve large-scale modification of global weather patterns through focused ionospheric disturbances.[18]

Two thousand years ago the prophet John warned that in the last days there would be unprecedented destruction from the sun and the sky that would afflict the rebellious humanity living during the seven-year Tribulation period leading up to Armageddon and the return of Christ: "And the fourth angel poured out his vial upon the sun; and power was given unto him to scorch men with fire. And men were scorched with great heat, and blasphemed the name of God, which hath power over these plagues: and they repented not to give him glory" (Revelation 16:8–9).

It is possible that weather modification technology in the hands of competing military alliances of the Western-based Antichrist and the kings of the east during the cataclysmic conflict of the last days could unleash the destruction foretold by the prophet of God. Remarkably, there are reports that HAARP technology can create explosions equivalent in power to those produced with nuclear weapons, but without producing nuclear radiation.[19]

HAARP transmitters can also send an enormous burst of electromagnetic radiation toward the ionosphere and reflect the radiation back to earth directly on an enemy target. In a controlled pattern, this radiation would cause enormous destruction. Further, several reports suggest that this technology also has the ability to create an impenetrable electromagnetic shield over a nation to prevent incoming enemy missiles, bombers, or other weapons from entering its airspace.[20]

GENETIC WEAPONS OF THE FUTURE

Advances in mapping the human genome have produced the devastating potential of creating a specially tailored disease targeted at a particular race, such as the race of an enemy nation. In addition, because every individual has unique DNA, there is the theoretical possibility that weapons could be created to target a specific person's genetic profile. An enemy nation's president and other high officials could be singled out for death. This diabolical possibility of individually targeted genetic weapons was explored in Robert Ludlum's novel *The Moscow Vector*.[21]

An article in the *India Daily* described the danger to humanity that could emerge from new understandings of the human genome: "If a genetic bomb was developed, it could contain anthrax or the plague and be tailored to activate when it identified a certain group of genes—indicating membership of a particular ethnic group—in the infected person.... The genetic warfare has started silently. Scientists are trying to understand how genetic characteristics can be used to trigger viral agents."[22]

A much more deadly threat arises from the possibility that scientists might develop genocidal weapons of mass destruction, targeting specific populations that represent a threat to the ruling powers. This could lead to the mass destruction of entire populations. It is possible that genetic warfare may be one of the horrors of the seven-year Tribulation period referred to in Daniel's and John's prophecies (see Daniel 9:26–27; Revelation 6–18).[23]

BULLETPROOF CLOTHING

Bulletproof and knifeproof vests armored with Kevlar have been available to soldiers and SWAT team members for years. They have usually been uncomfortable, heavy, and often ineffective. However, Miguel Caballero, a Colombian clothing designer, supplies his customers with tailored, bulletproof suits, jackets, coats, and even dresses. To protect the wearer from violent attack, the clothing incorporates Caballero's bullet-resistant material, which he claims is capable of stopping a bullet from a nine-millimeter pistol. Credible private reports state that President Obama wore a similar bullet-resistant suit throughout the 2009 inauguration ceremonies at the request of the Secret Service.[24]

AN ADVANCED BULLET-TRACKING DEVICE

A new police and military surveillance system makes it possible to track the path of a bullet after it is fired. Specialized television cameras track in real time the path of a bullet traveling up to fourteen hundred feet per second. Then a computer system backtracks the bullet's path to determine its point of origin. A SWAT sniper can then fire at the enemy gunman using a telescopic rifle aimed at the location as determined by the computer.[25] A parallel system uses microphones to track the sound and locate the source of a shot after it is fired.[26]

ELECTRONIC CAMOUFLAGE SYSTEM

New military technology includes electronic camouflage devices that alter the perceived appearance of military vehicles, causing them to appear to match the colors and textures in the background. This technique makes a lightly armored vehicle virtually invisible to the naked eye from a distance. Cameras record the elements that exist in the background, such as sand, earth, and vegetation, then electronically project these visual images on the surface of the vehicle that is facing enemy combatants. The observers see what is behind the vehicle, causing the vehicle to virtually disappear.

NANOTECHNOLOGY AND NUCLEAR WEAPONS

The miniaturizing of nuclear weapons has led to microfusion bombs. A powerful range of military nanotechnology weapons has been developed, including micro, low-yield nuclear weapons. The United States, the United Kingdom, France, Russia, and China (probably Israel as well) have the capacity to deploy mini-nuclear weapons, which produce precise but devastating effects against any enemy target.[27]

Developments in weapons technology, such as those discussed in this chapter, will play a large role in establishing the military domination of the Western forces of the Antichrist during the initial part of the seven-year Tribulation. However, many of these weapons may also be used by the kings of the east, probably including China, India, and Japan—the nations of Asia desperate to throw off the shackles of the Antichrist's Western-based domination. At the end of the Antichrist's period of global domination, a titanic battle will be waged between the enormous armies of the East and the armies of the West, led by the Antichrist.

In chapter 12 we will examine the prophecies that describe the astonishing outcome of that final global war, culminating in the battle of Armageddon, when Jesus Christ will return to save Israel from annihilation. Christ will defeat His enemies and set up His Millennial Kingdom on earth. Finally, humanity will experience true peace, freedom from violence and oppression, and the establishment of a righteous and just government under the Messiah.

PART 3

POLITICAL PLANS FOR GLOBAL GOVERNMENT

CHAPTER 7

LEADING CONSPIRATORS IN ADVANCING THE GLOBALIST AGENDA

Exposing the Elite's Secret Plans to Control the Future World Government

A number of groups are working tirelessly—mostly behind the scenes but occasionally in the open—to centralize the governing authority for the entire world. Students of prophecy, as well as those who value democratic, national, sovereign governments, know how sinister these efforts are, and many will wonder why public officeholders, former high-ranking government officials, extremely wealthy businessmen, and others would devote their expertise to such a dark undertaking.

I believe that many of those who are working to create a global government are, in their own assessment, operating from a genuine and personally benevolent philosophical position. They feel that centralizing the ruling power will help protect billions of world citizens from the potential genocidal danger of nuclear, chemical, and biological warfare. You might think that the leaders of the shadow government are knowingly devoting their energies to advancing

Satan's agenda for political, economic, and military domination of the earth. However, I suspect, for most of them that is not the case.

Leaders of the globalist elite, as far as I can determine, embrace the goal of eliminating sovereign national governments because they believe a centralized world government would prevent the outbreak of a devastating world war. What they don't realize is that in helping to form the global government of the future Antichrist, they are putting in place the preconditions for a series of end-times battles leading to the final battle of Armageddon.

From the perspective of members of the globalist elite, there is good reason to work for a centralized world government. Following the genocidal devastation of World War II, with more than seventy million killed, many world leaders started looking for a different way to think about government. Added to the horrors of the World War II was the emergence of realistic end-of-the-world scenarios made plausible by the production of nuclear, biological, and chemical weapons. National leaders throughout the world came to believe that humanity was destined to experience total genocide in another world war.

With that in mind, a number of business and political leaders concluded that the "true leaders" of the Western world must secretly join together without the knowledge or direct permission of their governments or the support of their fellow citizens. They decided to create a secret global organization dedicated to eliminating the national sovereignty of all existing countries. Their plan was to replace the ancient system of independent nations with a global government.

For decades the globalist elite have been working to put in place the personnel, financing, and intergovernmental structures needed to supersede national governments with one global center of power. To bring this about, a multitude of billionaire business leaders, academic elites, and their political partners (often former senior government officials) have joined supersecret globalist organizations. These groups don't issue news releases to report on their progress, but there is every indication that the globalists have already implemented much of their agenda, moving ever closer to realizing their ultimate goal.

I refer to this unofficial regime as a shadow government because it forbids the release of any information and is closed to journalists who might report on their clandestine meetings. The elite have no interest either in disclosing their plans to the public or inviting public input. At the heart of the globalist agenda is an antidemocratic commitment to avoiding public scrutiny and public accountability and public opposition.

TWO FORMS OF SHADOW GOVERNMENT

Actually in this book I'm describing two types of shadow government. In addition to a global shadow government, there is a national shadow government, which exists to preserve the continuity of government plans—the personnel, facilities, and technology—during a time of overwhelming national crisis. This type of shadow government is absolutely necessary, and its sole purpose is to protect the nation, its form of government, and its citizens in times of military attack, terrorist acts, or overwhelming natural disasters.

This shadow government operates simultaneously with the elected government, and the parallel approach is designed to guarantee the survival and continuity of Western governments in the event of an attack that uses weapons of mass destruction. The idea is to protect citizens by protecting the vital departments of national government. To accomplish this, many of the leaders of national security must keep their identity invisible.

A report on the formation of a parallel government structure stated:

> The Continuity of Government (COG) program ensures the survival of essential federal government leaders and agencies in the event of a severe crisis.... COG...maintains underground facilities to protect the president, cabinet members, and essential government personnel in the event of attack or catastrophe....
>
> Intended to preserve the American form of representative government, continuity of federal authority aided law enforcement, ensured general safety, and protected the government from the illegal assumption of power by rival foreign powers or anti-government organizations. The government acknowledged plans to construct secret facilities and

implement a COG strategy, but the details and locations of COG operations were meant to remain secret.[1]

The shadow government in each nation maintains subterranean military bases and virtual cities designed to allow the continuity of vital government functions. Here is the description of one such site: "The Mount Weather Special Facility is a Continuity of Government (COG) facility operated by the Federal Emergency Management Agency (FEMA). The 200,000 square foot facility also houses FEMA's National Emergency Coordinating Center. Located on a 434 acre mountain site on the borders of Loudon and Clarke counties [Virginia], the above ground support facilities include about a dozen building[s] providing communications links to the White House Situation Room."[2]

From time to time reports appear about the existence of government installations built to resist nuclear attack. A large number of current and former cabinet members, senators, members of Congress, military leaders, and essential bureaucrats are selected in advance to be part of the parallel government. The well-respected journalist Seymour M. Hersh had this to say about facilities for the shadow governments in Russia and the United States: "The Soviet government began digging a huge underground complex outside Moscow. Analysts concluded that the underground facility was designed for 'continuity of government'—for the political and military leadership to survive a nuclear war. (There are similar facilities, in Virginia and Pennsylvania, for the American leadership.)"[3]

In the 1950s, President Dwight Eisenhower issued several secret presidential executive orders that authorized a shadow government of former senators, former congressmen, and former cabinet members to replace elected government leaders in the event that the elected government was destroyed. The names and identities of members of this government are top secret. To facilitate this shadow government, a complex network of duplicate computers, records, and other vital material has been established. This on-call government can take over the country at a moment's notice following a national disaster.

While every person who cherishes democratic freedoms desires that all government functions be as open as possible and subject to review in congressional or parliamentary committees, we live in a very different world today. We are all subject to the extreme danger posed by weapons systems in the hands of enemy and rogue nations and terror groups. As a resurgent Russia abandons democracy and begins reinstituting the Soviet Empire and as Middle Eastern governments and terrorists present a staggering global threat, a shadow government of national leaders is vital to the survival of a stable government.

For example, while the U.S. Senate, House of Representatives, members of the cabinet, President Obama, and Vice President Biden were fulfilling their constitutional responsibilities on Inauguration Day in 2009, our national leaders were assembled in one place and vulnerable to attack. Meanwhile, the shadow government was available and ready under the leadership of Secretary of Defense Robert Gates, the cabinet member selected for that role on that day. The shadow government was assembled at an undisclosed underground government headquarters.[4]

By contrast, the second type of shadow government poses an unprecedented threat to the rights, freedoms, and privacy of all citizens. The global elites who work behind the scenes to achieve a New World Order wish to subvert our national sovereignty, our independence, and our representative form of government. They are using international treaties and other tools to eliminate our national independence. The global elite want to install a government that will rule secretly behind boardroom doors to achieve goals that they are convinced would not be welcomed by citizens of free societies. That is why they protect the secrecy of membership lists as well as the agendas and proceedings of their meetings. I'm sure you join me in opposing these attempts to subvert the constitutions of Western democracies in ways that will destroy our independence, our freedom, and our privacy.

Unfortunately, the second type of shadow government inevitably uses the laws that were created to deal with legitimate national crises—including natural disasters and war—to their own antidemocratic ends.

A SHORT HISTORY OF GLOBALISM

Following the end of World War II, the individuals who controlled the greatest political and military power in Europe and North America quickly formed the shadow government. The leaders are virtually unknown individuals who, for the most part, have never been elected to public office in any country. They are known only to their associates in the rarified atmosphere of high finance, secret intelligence agencies, and senior military leadership, with a few former high-profile political leaders.

It might be difficult for an American citizen to fathom how a self-appointed group could achieve such power over world affairs. A brief comparison will help put this in perspective. Think for a moment about the global economic collapse in 2008. In an attempt by various national governments to reverse the slide, unprecedented amounts of money—trillions of dollars—were given in bailouts to banks, mutual funds, automakers, and major international corporations. And this was done largely without public debate, serious governmental oversight, or public reporting. We are witnessing a massive transfer of taxpayer funds to numerous private companies and organizations, most of whose leaders share a commitment to the globalist agenda.

Consider one of the leading thinkers whose philosophy promotes the ideal of world government. James Paul Warburg, a financier who wielded great influence in the U.S. government, declared before the U.S. Senate on February 7, 1950, "We shall have World Government, whether or not we like it. The only question is whether World Government will be achieved by conquest or consent."[5] He further stated, "A World Order without world law is an anachronism; and…since war now means the extinction of civilization, a world which fails to establish the rule of law over the nation-states cannot long continue to exist. We are living in a perilous period of transition from the era of the fully sovereign nation-state to the era of World Government."[6]

Recent moves toward socialism by the U.S. government are transferring America's free-enterprise economy to the control of the federal government. We have witnessed a government takeover of Wall Street investment organizations, major U.S. banks, the mortgage finance industry, the auto industry, and numerous other areas of the economy.

CREATING A WORLD GOVERNMENT POWERHOUSE

Nothing in the universe can resist the cumulative ardor of a sufficiently large number of enlightened minds working together in organized groups.—Pierre Teilhard de Chardin[7]

A century ago a fascinating intellectual writer by the name of John Buchan wrote a number of intriguing books, including the novels *The Thirty-Nine Steps* and *The Power-House.* Buchan later in life became a UK politician and was appointed in 1935 as the governor-general of Canada, representing the Queen as head of state. In *The Power-House,* Buchan described a curious new development of modern political power. He pointed out that the fall of numerous European royal families at the end of World War I had led to a tendency to obscure the identities and roles of those who truly wielded political power.

In the aftermath of governmental upheavals endured by Russia, Italy, Germany, and China, it was difficult even for Western intelligence specialists to discern who was truly in charge. The nature of modern governments is to camouflage those who control the significant levers of political and economic power. Even in the United States and Canada, the decades of military threats from Russia and China and the more recent dangers of terrorist attack have motivated Western nations to create shadow governments.

THE BILDERBERGER GROUP

It is one thing for nations to safeguard their people and their national integrity by forming a parallel government structure. But in Europe a self-appointed shadow government is busy setting up a framework that may be used as the basis of a world government. This secret European group, known as the Bilderbergers, has attracted elite members—notably financial, political, and military leaders—from every key nation. It is by far the most secretive of the private international councils working to achieve world government. In 1954 the political and financial leadership of postwar Europe gathered at the Hotel de Bilderberg in Oosterbeek, the Netherlands, to create the plans and solidify the relationships needed to unify the nations of Europe with the United States. This confederation of European nations would form a new empire for the first time since the days of ancient Rome. The group has been meeting since 1945 in top-secret gatherings. Although they are known publicly as the Bilderbergers, the members call their group the Alliance. Strict rules prohibit members from discussing any plans, speeches, and policies outside their secret meetings.

The Bilderberger group was initially financed by the Central Intelligence Agency and organized by U.S. Army Gen. Walter Bedell Smith. Founding members included Colin Gubbins, head of British intelligence; Stansfield Turner, director of the CIA; Henry Kissinger, former U.S. secretary of state; Lord Rothschild; and Lawrence Rockefeller. The Bilderbergers meet twice a year to consolidate their efforts to create the "United States of Europe" as well as to advance their ultimate plan for world government.[8]

During the last few decades, the Bilderbergers—along with powerful members of the globalist Council on Foreign Relations and the Trilateral Commission—have consolidated their control of the military, the economy, and the political arena throughout the governments of America, Canada, Europe, and Asia. The globalist planners admit, "The public and leaders of most countries continue to live in a mental universe which no longer exists—a world of separate nations—and have great difficulties thinking in terms of global perspectives and interdependence."[9]

The globalist elite realize that the vast majority of citizens love and support their own countries and will not easily give up national sovereignty and independence. Fear is one motivator being used to break down loyalty to one's country. President George H. W. Bush explained that global government could not be achieved unless some great international public crisis motivated the population to abandon their attachment to national sovereignty. He warned, "From chaos will emerge the New World Order."[10]

The great English historian Arnold Toynbee observed the terrible devastation caused by the great wars during the last century. He then concluded in his book *Surviving the Future* that it was essential that a powerful world government be formed to prevent the extinction of humanity:

> We are approaching the point at which the only effective scale for operations of any importance will be the global scale. The local states ought to be deprived of their sovereignty and subordinated to the sovereignty of a global world government. I think the world state will still need an armed police [and the] world government will have to command sufficient force to be able to impose peace.... The people of each local sovereign state will have to renounce their state's sovereignty and subordinate it to the paramount sovereignty of a literally worldwide world government.

Toynbee added, "I want to see a world government established."[11]

The historian's words regarding the need for world government are no longer considered revolutionary. Unfortunately, Toynbee's rejection of the value and need for sovereign nation-states to preserve democracy, freedom, and culture is now shared by many individuals in the financial, political, and media elite. These leaders and trendsetters see themselves as world citizens rather than as Americans or Canadians or Britons or Germans. They are planning to create a literal New World Order.

The Bible revealed that in the ancient past before the Flood, all the peoples on earth lived as one community sharing a common language. However, the unrighteous people of that day joined together to defy God by creating an engineering feat: the Tower of Babel in ancient Mesopotamia. The Lord intervened and miraculously confused the language of millions of people, preventing them from communicating with or understanding one another. By creating a multitude of new languages, the Lord forced the human population to separate into individual language groupings. As a result of God's intervention, the first language groupings and the resulting ethnic groups were created. This reveals that the nation-state is part of God's long-term plan to preserve cultural diversity and identity. It is interesting to note that John prophesied that individual nations will still exist in the New Earth during the Millennium and beyond. "And the nations of them which are saved shall walk in the light of it [the New Jerusalem]: and the kings of the earth do bring their glory and honour into it" (Revelation 21:24).

But those who support the New World Order want to unite every nation into a global government. Zbigniew Brzezinski, the former national security advisor to President Jimmy Carter and a founding member of the Trilateral Commission, wrote the book *Between Two Ages,* which argued in favor of the need for a world government. Brzezinski wrote, "National sovereignty is no longer a viable concept."[12]

Realizing that the patriotism of millions of citizens of independent nations would prove to be a serious and perhaps impossible obstacle to the achievement of globalist plans, Brzezinski suggested that plans for world government could best be achieved through gradual "movement toward a larger community of developed nations…through a variety of indirect ties and already-developing limitations on national sovereignty."[13]

In other words, those who want to destroy the sovereignty of the United States and Canada have determined to create world government incrementally and by stealth, without political debate or democratic agreement.

THE COUNCIL ON FOREIGN RELATIONS

The Council on Foreign Relations was established following World War I in an attempt to ensure that the financial and political life of the United States and Britain would support a foreign policy in line with the two countries' global interests. The organization has described its methods and goals as follows: "In speaking of public enlightenment, it is well to bear in mind that the Council has chosen as its function the enlightenment of the leaders of opinion. These, in turn, each in his own sphere, spread the knowledge gained here in ever-widening circles."[14]

The list of major, well-known corporate leaders, politicians, and media figures who are members of the council is staggering. And beyond membership in the Council on Foreign Relations, there is a subset of key players that claims interlocking membership in the Trilateral Commission as well as the Bilderberg group, composed of key individuals from international banking and manufacturing corporations, high-ranking military leaders, powerful U.S. diplomats, and cabinet members.[15] Few people make it into the inner circles of political power in Washington unless they have first served as invited members of the Council on Foreign Relations or the Trilateral Commission.

The Council on Foreign Relations is committed to the elimination of national borders and national sovereignty. Its members advocate merging all nations into one centralized, unrivaled world government. Members of the council and their globalist allies in other nations have shaped the economic, foreign-relations, and defense policies of the United States, Britain, France, Canada, Japan, and Germany for the last ninety years. The purpose of the Trilateral Commission and the Council on Foreign Relations is to infiltrate the decision-making bodies of government, education, business, the military, and the media. In doing so, they influence leaders in each key area to adopt and promote a globalist philosophy. By influencing leaders who remain officially outside the movement, they can more quickly accomplish the goal of a New World Order.

It has been publicly reported that Presidents Richard Nixon, Gerald Ford, Jimmy Carter, George H. W. Bush, and Bill Clinton were members of the Council on Foreign Relations. Most of these men also were members of the Trilateral Commission. When an individual is elected president or appointed to the cabinet, he or she usually resigns from the Council on Foreign Relations and/or the Trilateral Commission while in office. Normally they resume their membership when they leave government service.

Presidential elections have been reduced to popularity polls because citizens are given only two major-party choices: Democrat Team A or Republican Team B. The teams wear different-colored sweaters, but the hidden management and ownership and players are virtually identical. Most cabinet members, senior military staff, and State Department officials in every administration are also members of the Council on Foreign Relations or the Trilateral Commission. Several Internet sites allege that a great number of key business, education, and political leaders in America are or have been members of the council.[16]

President Ronald Reagan's administration included at least 225 members of the globalist organizations. George H. W. Bush's administration was overwhelmingly represented by members of the two groups, including almost every member of the cabinet. When President Clinton took office, virtually every officer of his cabinet and subcabinet was drawn from members of these two globalist groups. The same situation existed during the eight years of George W. Bush's administration,[17] and in all likelihood the pattern will continue in the administration of President Obama.

THE TRILATERAL COMMISSION

The Trilateral Commission (the "three sides" being North America, Europe, and Japan) funds studies, networks hundreds of their people into the White House and the State Department, and builds relationships with other one-world-government groups in Britain and Europe. Zbigniew Brzezinski, the national security advisor to President Carter, and David Rockefeller—both key members of the Council on Foreign Relations—created the Trilateral Commission in 1973. The commission's declared purpose is to achieve "close trilateral cooperation" in "keeping the peace, managing the world economy," "fostering economic development," and alleviating "world poverty," which "will improve the chances of a smooth and peaceful evolution of the global system."[18]

The nature and goals of the Trilateral Commission became publicly known during President Carter's administration. The news media discovered that many of Carter's highest officials and cabinet members belonged to this group, including Carter himself, Vice President Walter Mondale, and CIA Director Stansfield Turner. An article in *Millennium—Journal of International Studies* reported, "Although the [Trilateral] Commission's primary concern is economic, the Trilateralists pinpointed a vital political objective: to gain control of the American presidency."[19]

The Trilateral Commission has brought together powerbrokers from the military, politics, finance, and business from vital geographical spheres. The United States, Russia, China, Japan, South Korea, Taiwan, Singapore, and the European Union are now the dominant powers in key globalist groups.[20]

The Trilateral Commision's plan requires that the three geopolitical super-powers (North America, Europe, and Japan) create a political, military, and economic alliance to dominate neighboring countries in their spheres. Once they consolidate geopolitical and military control in their respective regions, the final step will be to merge the three spheres of geopolitical power into a one-world government.

Regardless of whether the White House is in the hands of Republicans or Democrats, the true power that rules America is concentrated in the hands of several thousand individuals who have been chosen from key areas of American society to join the globalist elite. They cannot hold a primary allegiance to the U.S. Constitution and its principles of American sovereignty as an independent democratic nation. Instead, they are committed to the creation of a global government, with national borders no longer having any true meaning.

INTERNATIONAL INSTITUTIONS AND THE COMING WORLD GOVERNMENT

While much of the work of the globalist elite takes place in secret, a number of public institutions openly push the globalist agenda. The United Nations (UN), the North Atlantic Treaty Organization (NATO), the World Trade Organization (WTO), and the International Monetary Fund (IMF) are among the major institutions that promote a system favorable to one-world government. A key element of the long-range strategy is a plan to centralize control of international finance. In the future if a country turns to the IMF and the World Bank for financial assistance, they will be required to essentially abandon their national sovereignty. The IMF and the World Bank are counting on a global financial collapse to trigger an international crisis that will enable them to seize control of the nations' currencies and economies in preparation for global governance.[21]

The Ford Foundation financed a provocative study called *Renewing the United Nations System*, written by two former UN officials, Sir Brian Urquhart and Erskine Childers. The study recommended significant changes to streamline and strengthen UN operations and suggested that the UN General Assembly, the Security Council, the IMF, the World Health Organization, and the International Labor Organization be transferred to one central location, possibly Bonn or New York, to improve efficiency and centralize political control. The authors also recommended the abolition of the current weighted voting system of the IMF, which permits the superpowers to dictate policy. The report's proposal introduced a radical voting system that would allow third world nations to dictate where and when loans would be granted from wealthy countries to poorer ones.[22]

It is obvious that this proposal was intended to lay the foundation for a one-world government. Consider the wording: "While there is no question, at present, of the transformation of the UN system into a supranational authority, the organization is in a transitional phase, basically shaped and constrained by national sovereignty, but sometimes acting outside and beyond it."[23]

Notice the provocative use of the phrase "at present." This document in its entirety refers to "gradual limitation of sovereignty," "notable abridgements of national sovereignty," "chipping away at the edges of traditional sovereignty," and "small steps towards an eventual trans-sovereign society." The authors discussed their globalist plans to erode, and then replace, our nation's cherished sovereignty. However, they recommended that the transition proceed gradually so as not to alarm the patriotic citizens of Western democracies.

The report recommended significant steps to achieve world government. The authors discussed interim steps that must be taken "until the world is ready for world government." The report suggested that the UN should independently raise funds for its own budget by assessing a global surcharge tax on "all arms sales," on "all transnational movement of currencies," on "all international trade: or on the production of such specific materials as petroleum," and "a United Nations levy on international air and sea travel."[24]

Other recommendations included assessing a "one day" annual income tax on every person in the world. This taxation proposal is a key indication of the gradual transformation of the UN from international consultative body of member states to the creation of a global superstate. The UN has also called for a global tax to be used to reduce government deficits and stimulate economic activity. This incredible proposal represents a major step toward the coming world government. If the UN could generate its own tax revenue, it would no longer be dependent on political and financial support from member states.

The report also proposed a series of political steps required to establish a world government, making the UN the nucleus of a future world government. There is a huge difference between the present UN system, which is an assembly of representatives of national governments, and the plan described in *Renewing the United Nations System,* which would have parliamentarians elected by all citizens on the planet. Using the example of the European Parliament, which is made up of elected representatives of the citizens of the European Union member nations, many globalists have called for a "world people's assembly."[25]

The UN's third annual report, dated January 17, 2006, "provides comprehensive analysis of the world's progress towards realizing the UN's Millennium Development Goals [toward global government], endorsed by leaders of 189 countries in 2000." The report concluded, "While global efforts to reach the UN Millennium Development Goals improved on some fronts in 2005, the world is still investing less than half the effort needed. While there was progress in the areas of peace and security, poverty, hunger, health, and education, efforts in the environment and human rights slipped backwards."[26]

The former leader of the USSR, Mikhail Gorbachev, worked as spokesperson for a number of world government groups. Gorbachev called for the creation of regional security councils to work toward world government under a mandate from the UN. In 1993 Gorbachev wrote a column, which was republished by the *New York Times,* stating that there was an urgent need for

a European Security Council, a Secretary General for Europe, structures that have authority and a collective mandate, plus military forces for prevention of future crises and for rapid deployment when necessary....

Many of today's tragedies are born from the absolute ascendancy given to national sovereignty. People have the right to their identity, culture, and language. But to carry this principle beyond the bounds of reason mires us in problems that no one can solve.[27]

THE INTERNATIONAL CRIMINAL COURT

In 2002 the International Criminal Court (ICC) was established in The Hague, the Netherlands. The court tries soldiers, anywhere in the world, who are accused of war crimes. The existing International Court of Justice, often called the World Court, is also at The Hague. However, the International Court of Justice rules only on disputes between sovereign states.

As of January 2009, 108 nations had signed the International Criminal Court Treaty regarding the handling of war crimes. The treaty is a major step toward the globalization of criminal law. Concern arose in the U.S. Senate that the court's statutes would permit the arrest and trial of American soldiers and U.S. civilians who are on active government duty around the world.[28] As a result of these concerns, American and Israeli representatives "unsigned" the treaty, withdrawing from the ICC.[29]

The work of the Trilateral Commission, the Bilderberger group, and the Council on Foreign Relations—together with developments at the UN and other international institutions—gives us reason to pay much closer attention to the prophecies of Daniel and John. The agenda of the globalist elite is consistent with what we read in Scripture about the coming rule of the Antichrist. We will explore that in greater detail in chapters 9 and 10.

CHAPTER 8

GLOBALISTS WANT TO CONTROL THE INFORMATION YOU RECEIVE

Major News Media Tell You Only What They Think You Should Know

As we have seen, secret groups are working on multiple fronts to create a centralized, autonomous world government. The preparations for this ultimate goal reach into even news-gathering organizations.

Major multinational communications conglomerates control most of the national and international news media, and the major media regularly restrict coverage of important political, military, intelligence, and financial stories. Much of what happens in the world—issues and events that affect our lives and our future—is never reported. Deeper issues related to the Middle East conflict and developments in Russia, China, and other nations where freedom of the press is restricted are hardly ever reported in the West.

Many people feel that the natural competition between media outlets will ensure that at least a few major outlets will aggressively cover and report the important stories from around the world. However, even in nations where freedom of the press is guaranteed, the media are seldom allowed to operate freely.

The most powerful men and women in the world have been meeting in secret conclaves every year for more than half a century, and the proceedings of their meetings are never reported in depth by any major news-gathering operation. The Bilderberger Group, the Trilateral Commission, and the Council on Foreign Relations continue to meet behind closed doors, with no major news media attempting to crack their secrecy.

In this chapter we will look at a number of stories and developments that have a direct bearing on your life but which have not been considered newsworthy by the major media. It is vital that we understand what is going on behind the headlines and that we realize the types of stories that are regularly suppressed. In the endnotes for this chapter, I identify a number of useful research sources on the Internet. These sources confirm the information I am highlighting. In each case I have independently confirmed the accuracy of this fascinating research with intelligence and military sources in the Middle East and Asia.

THE ATTEMPTED DIRTY ATOMIC BOMB ATTACK ON ISRAEL

With Somalia descending into chaos with no functioning government and the only authority being various competing Islamic warlords, thousands of Somalis have found piracy to be very lucrative. Tens of thousands of merchant vessels travel along the coast of Somalia on their way to Europe through the Suez Canal. They are vulnerable to attack as they pass through the narrow strait that leads from the Indian Ocean through the Gulf of Aden into the Red Sea. Somalia's eighteen-hundred-mile-long coastline borders this strategic sea lane. A significant portion of the world's commercial sea traffic (including oil tankers) must traverse this dangerous seaway through the Suez Canal and onward through the Mediterranean Sea to reach the hundreds of ports of the European Union.

Major media outlets have reported on the dramatic increase in acts of piracy off the coast of Somalia. However, they have failed to report on some of the cargo aboard a ship that one group of pirates attacked. On August 21, 2008, between southern Yemen and Somalia near the Horn of Africa, pirates intercepted the Iranian ship *Iran Deyanat*. This container ship was boarded by twenty-five pirates armed with AK-47 assault rifles and rocket-propelled grenade launchers. The ship had set sail from Nanjing, China, on July 28, 2008, supposedly headed for the port of Rotterdam in the Netherlands. The ship is owned and operated by the Islamic Republic of Iran Shipping Lines (IRISL), a state-owned company run by the Iranian military. The cargo was officially listed as normal commodities, including 42,500 tons of metal ore and machinery. However, the U.S. Coast Guard has revealed that Iran routinely falsifies its shipping manifests to disguise not only the cargo but also the ultimate destination of its shipments. In this way Iran has been transporting illegal weapons and other contraband.

The captain of the *Iran Deyanat* had no choice but to submit to the well-armed pirates who boarded his ship in August 2008. The Somalis were members of a crime syndicate based in Eyl, a small fishing village now transformed into a pirate haven in northern Somalia. The Somali pirates are, to their way of thinking, running a normal business in which they capture ships and then offer to release the crew and ship in exchange for a ransom. Ransoms have averaged $2.5 million per ship unless the ship is much larger or the cargo is more valuable than most. In the case of the *Iran Deyanat*, leaders of the band of pirates were engaged in ransom negotiations. At the same time, members of the pirate crew began to grow sick with terrible skin eruptions and hair loss. By September 1, 2008, sixteen pirates were dead. The others were covered with burns and suffered hair loss, nausea, and other signs of radiation sickness.[1] According to the *Times* newspaper of Johannesburg, South Africa, the original twenty-five Somali pirates who boarded the *Iran Deyanat* began dying from a "mysterious illness."[2]

The captured ship was taken to the harbor at Eyl, on the eastern coast of Somalia. The Somali minister of minerals and oil, Hassan Osman, sent a delegation to Eyl in an attempt to negotiate the ship's release. Osman stated later that during the week when his team was negotiating with the pirates, many of the pirates showed signs of sickness and soon died. It was also noted that Iranian crew members were not willing to reveal the true nature of the ship's cargo.[3]

Eventually, twenty-two of the twenty-five pirates died. The pirates had penetrated one of the cargo containers to check for valuable cargo that would give them reason to up the ante in their ransom negotiations. Negotiators realized that the pirated cargo was not typical commercial cargo and not even a load of illegal conventional weapons. American negotiators suspected it was radioactive material, based on the medical symptoms of the dying pirates. They offered the pirates up to seven million dollars to allow the Americans to board the ship and inspect the cargo. The cargo was found to be a large amount of uranium, transported in sandy gravel and surrounded by an extraordinary amount of explosives. The Iranian-owned ship contained the largest dirty atomic bombs ever conceived, and they were targeted against Israel. No source has revealed to this point how U.S. negotiators became involved.

An interrogation of the ship's officers revealed that had they not been intercepted by pirates, they would have traveled through the Suez Canal and entered the Mediterranean Sea on their supposed route to Rotterdam. However, the secret plan was that the ship's captain would declare a false marine emergency and request permission to enter a major Israeli harbor, such as Haifa or Ashdod, for emergency repairs. When he got the ship within range, the captain would abandon the vessel and activate a remote trigger to detonate a massive explosion of radioactive material into the atmosphere over the harbor and the adjoining seaport. The attack was scheduled for Yom Kippur, October 9, 2008.[4]

If the evil Iranian plot had not been stopped by the grace of God, the explosive release of radioactive material would likely have killed more than ten thousand Jews and Arabs in the targeted city. In addition, the resulting radioactive material, carried on the winds over the city and neighboring areas, would have killed hundreds of thousands of Jews and Arabs during the following decade. The port city would probably have registered dangerous levels of radioactivity for up to a century afterward.

Consider the international incident that would have followed such an attack. If Iran had detonated a dirty atomic bomb in a major Israeli harbor, Israel would have been forced to retaliate—possibly wiping out Iran. The world escaped a Middle Eastern nuclear war solely due to the providence of God.

A NUCLEAR EARTHQUAKE IN CHINA

A devastating earthquake occurred on May 12, 2008, in the central Sichuan Province of China. It registered 8.1 on the Richter scale, initially killing approximately ten thousand citizens and destroying their homes. The earthquake seriously injured at least a quarter of a million people. The Chinese media revealed on May 31, 2008, that a serious nuclear accident had occurred on May 12 in the mountainous area of Sichuan Province. Although Chinese authorities initially declared that only ten thousand citizens had died, it was revealed later that more than sixty thousand died during this disaster.

However, a debate over the number of dead was not the biggest issue related to this story. Many Chinese citizens who witnessed the event reported their uncensored observations over the Internet to relatives and friends living outside the country. These citizens said that the explosion was not initially an earthquake but some other underground disturbance. They described an extraordinary appearance of what seemed to be white magma flowing from an enormous hole at the summit of a mountain. Since the mountains in that region are composed of granite and not volcanic material, the observers knew the material could not be volcanic magma. The eyewitnesses concluded that the massive emission of material from the mountain must have come from enormous subterranean military bases they knew existed beneath the surface of the Sichuan mountains. The curious nature of the released material showed that a phenomenal amount of concrete particles were emitted from inside the mountain. These were originally part of the concrete that the People's Liberation Army (PLA) is known to use to build underground military bases and virtual cities. One such underground facility houses China's largest nuclear reactor, a warhead assembly plant, and a major warhead storage armory.

One report declared that "Mr. He, a local resident, stated that when the earthquake occurred on May 12, people saw something erupt from the top of a mountain next to the valley, 'It looked like toothpaste being squeezed out,' said He. It was these concrete pieces. The eruption lasted about three minutes."[5]

The China News Services (CNS) reported on May 31, 2008, that military paramedics from PLA hospitals discovered that enormous concrete blocks and pulverized concrete debris had filled the bottom of a valley close to the blast's epicenter. Citizen observers reported that the mountain had blown up, leaving an enormous hole on the side of the mountain near its peak. Reports said material poured down the side of the mountain and filled the valley below with a stream of molten material one and a half miles long.

Internet reports from China reveal that the nature and thickness of the concrete pieces found in the valley matched those used by the PLA in the construction of deep-underground nuclear bases. A report posted at the *Epoch Times* revealed the following: "According to a China News Services (CNS) report on May 31, 2008, paramedics from People's Liberation Army (PLA) hospitals and psychologists from Beijing onsite May 23 found concrete debris at the bottom of a valley near the epicenter. The half-mile-wide valley was covered with debris 10–20 inches thick, covering the valley floor for almost 1.5 miles."[6] Chinese earthquake experts examined the valley that was filled with unusual concrete debris. Local residents reported that military personnel in protective suits headed into the area.[7]

While Chinese authorities initially claimed an earthquake destroyed the underground facility, it is known that this subterranean base is used for nuclear warhead production, assembly, and storage. The best evidence strongly suggests that a massive nuclear explosion occurred in China's most vital nuclear base and may well have destroyed a significant portion of China's nuclear arsenal. Eight seconds later the earthquake occurred.

Recently a senior Chinese army source secretly reported to Western authorities that the Sichuan earthquake triggered a chain reaction of nuclear explosions in the Sichuan mountain areas. The explosions inevitably destroyed a significant portion of the PLA's largest nuclear reactor, its nuclear warhead assembly plant, and its major nuclear warhead storage site, together with new weapons-testing laboratories. The Chinese military tightly controls its nuclear warhead inventory by retaining the warheads and the arming codes primarily in this top-secret subterranean nuclear armory.[8]

Chinese news sources on the Internet revealed that the Chinese military had admitted that twenty-seven hundred chemical cleanup workers were sent to the Sichuan earthquake area for nuclear/chemical emergency rescue. CNS reported that earthquake experts had completed a seismic analysis and had suggested that a nuclear explosion might have occurred at the Sichuan epicenter. Official Chinese military sources initially suggested that their readings revealed a huge explosion of a large-scale military armory in Sichuan.

International earthquake observers and military scientists throughout Southeast Asia confirmed that an enormous, earthshaking event occurred just seconds before the earthquake's epicenter was identified. The energy released was equivalent to that of a massive underground nuclear explosion. Scientists concluded that an accidental nuclear explosion triggered the earthquake. (The Chinese government suggested that the sequence happened in the reverse order, that an earthquake had triggered a nuclear explosion.[9])

The numerous reports that contradict the official Chinese explanation have not been publicly denied by China. However, accounts that varied from the official government reports did not originate with major news media organizations.

The story of a major nuclear accident in China and the report of a dirty atomic bomb being transported on an Iranian ship both point to a troubling trend. News media outlets want to control what you learn about world developments that have a bearing on your life. The control of information, especially information that the globalists want to hide, is a crucial component in their strategy to establish a one-world government.

CHAPTER 9

THE REVIVED ROMAN EMPIRE— THE EUROPEAN UNION

Prophecies That Are Being Fulfilled Today in Europe

More than five hundred years before the birth of the Roman Empire, the Old Testament prophets predicted the rise of an empire that would become the greatest empire the world had ever seen. Daniel proclaimed, "And the fourth kingdom shall be strong as iron: forasmuch as iron breaketh in pieces and subdueth all things: and as iron that breaketh all these, shall it break in pieces and bruise" (Daniel 2:40). Rome was destined to conquer every nation that stood in its path. However, when Daniel wrote his divinely inspired prophecy (approximately 580 B.C.), Rome was a small city-state of little consequence—even in the local Italian peninsula. Without divine inspiration, it would have been impossible for anyone to predict that this city-state would rise from obscurity to rule the world for more than a thousand years.

THE WORLD'S FIRST SUPERSTATE

In 66–63 B.C., the legions of the Roman general Pompey the Great conquered Syria and Judea, including Jerusalem. During Pompey's siege of Jerusalem, the legions slaughtered twelve thousand Judean soldiers in the final assault on the city. Jewish historical records indicate that the blood of the defenders of the Temple Mount in Jerusalem rose as high as a man's ankles in the Court of the Israelites. The Jews fought desperately against Pompey's troops as the pagan soldiers entered the sacred holy place.[1] From 63 B.C., Rome ruled over Israel.

Caesar Augustus ruled as emperor of Rome during the early life of Jesus Christ. During that period and for the following century, Roman legions expanded the empire to add the territories of what are now Egypt, Romania, Bulgaria, Hungary, Bosnia, Herzegovina, Croatia, and Serbia. Rome also dominated northern Europe, including the newly acquired territories of what are now England, Switzerland, Germany, northern France, and Belgium. No other empire had ruled so vast a geographical territory for such a long period of time. Rome exercised unrivaled military and political control over a hundred million subjects in an empire that extended more than a thousand miles from the western coasts of Britain and Spain to the eastern edges of the deserts of Arabia.

In A.D. 476 when the Western Roman Empire was conquered by waves of barbarian Germanic invaders, an enormous military vacuum was created in Europe. Rome's destruction set the stage for the Dark Ages, characterized by almost a thousand years of intellectual, religious, economic, and military chaos. However, the Eastern Roman Empire, based in Constantinople (now Istanbul, Turkey), continued to rule the eastern Mediterranean as well as parts of Sicily, Italy, northern Africa, and Spain. The Eastern Roman Empire continued for another thousand years until it fell to Muslim invaders in A.D. 1453.

Most other conquering empires in history absorbed the culture, tradition, and technologies of the peoples they conquered. The Roman Empire was distinct, however, in that it required its governors to crush the laws, religion, language, and society of every conquered nation. Rome replaced existing cultures with Roman laws and culture. Centuries have passed since the time of Rome's unrivaled power, yet the impact of Rome on subsequent Western societies and their history is unprecedented. After thousands of years, Europe, the Middle East, and even North America have retained forms of government, language, culture, and laws derived from those of ancient Rome.

JEWISH EXPECTATIONS ABOUT THE ANTICHRIST

The biblical prophets predicted that Rome would rise again to world dominance at the end of the age. That is happening today as the European Union, a confederation of nations covering the geography of ancient Rome, is setting the stage to become a dominant world empire.

The ancient Jews saw in their Scriptures a prophecy about a future satanic world ruler. This ruler, named the Antichrist in the New Testament, would arise to lead the reemergence of the Roman Empire as an unrivaled world power. Philo was a famous first-century Jewish writer living in Egypt. He wrote that the Antichrist would arise during the last days to oppress Israel. This would take place in the final generation before the return of the Messiah. In his book *On Rewards and Punishments,* Philo declared, "For a man will come forth, says the prophecy [Septuagint Greek translation of Numbers 24:7], who will go out and conduct a great war, and will overcome a great and powerful nation, as God Himself will assist His saints."[2]

The book of Zerubbabel, an apocryphal volume written by an unknown Jewish author, includes a reference to the Antichrist using the name Armillus. This name was related to the name Romulus, suggesting a strong connection with Rome. A number of early Targums (Jewish interpretive paraphrases of Old Testament passages) and commentaries on books of the Old Testament also identified Daniel's "prince that shall come" (Daniel 9:26) as the future leader of the revived Roman Empire. Daniel had prophesied, "The people of the prince that shall come shall destroy the city and the sanctuary; and the end thereof shall be with a flood, and unto the end of the war desolations are determined" (Daniel 9:26). Since the "people" who destroyed Jerusalem and the Temple sanctuary in A.D. 70 were the Romans, many of the ancient Jewish sages taught that Israel's last great enemy would arise from the revived Roman Empire.

One of the greatest tragedies in Israel's history occurred during the Jews' rebellion in A.D. 135 when the Roman emperor Hadrian killed more than one and a half million Jewish soldiers and civilians. The bloodshed occurred when Hadrian defeated the armies of the Jewish general Simeon Bar Kochba, who had declared that he was the messiah. On the ninth day of the Hebrew month of Av (August), A.D. 135, Bar Kochba lost a three-year war of independence waged against Rome. Several Israeli rabbis have spoken to me privately about their belief that the "spirit of Hadrian" will return in the last days. He will battle against Israel until he is defeated by the coming Messiah. Again, this belief ties the Antichrist to a revived Roman Empire.

Jewish sages have debated for centuries about the precise time when the long-awaited Messiah will appear. Some wrote that every Jew living in Israel needs to repent at one single moment to move God to send the long-prophesied Redeemer. The ancient rabbis wrote in the Talmud about the time when the Messiah will appear:

> All the predestined dates have passed and the matter [of Messiah's coming] depends only on repentance and good deeds.... Rabbi Joshua said: If they do not repent, will they not be redeemed? But the Holy One blessed be He, will set up a king over them, whose decrees shall be as cruel as Haman's whereby Israel shall engage in repentance, and he will then bring them back to the right path.[3]

This Jewish prophetic interpretation of a coming evil king suggests that God will use the evil king to finally bring Israel to repentance. The rabbis taught that the prophesied "king" would be "as cruel as Haman," the ancient Persian enemy who tried, but failed, to destroy all the Jews throughout the Persian Empire (see Esther 3–9). This rabbinic interpretation parallels the Christian prophetic commentaries regarding Daniel's prophecy that God will allow the Antichrist to come to global power to rule over Israel in order to bring the Jews to repentance.

FAILED ATTEMPTS TO REVIVE THE ROMAN EMPIRE

Daniel prophesied the revival of the fourth world empire in the days preceding the coming of the Messiah. Twenty-five centuries ago he wrote:

After this I saw in the night visions, and behold a fourth beast, dreadful
and terrible, and strong exceedingly; and it had great iron teeth: it
devoured and brake in pieces, and stamped the residue with the feet
of it: and it was diverse from all the beasts that were before it; and it
had ten horns. I considered the horns, and, behold, there came up
among them another little horn, before whom there were three of the
first horns plucked up by the roots: and, behold, in this horn were eyes
like the eyes of man, and a mouth speaking great things. (Daniel 7:7–8)

Once again the Roman Empire will take its place on the stage of world history as the dominant world power. Daniel also predicted that the restoration of
the empire would come in an unprecedented form, that of a superstate confederacy composed of ten nations. The confederacy would cover the territory of the
ancient Roman Empire—Western Europe and the nations surrounding the
Mediterranean Sea. A powerful dictator, the "little horn," will rise to rule the
empire by defeating three of the confederate nations and then seizing power
over all ten nations.

From the time of the disintegration of the Western Roman Empire in A.D.
476 until the closing days of World War II, the peoples of Europe, the Middle
East, and northern Africa have experienced violent struggles. Warfare continued
between the nation-states of Europe that grew out of the ancient provinces of
the Roman Empire. Through the following centuries, a number of political,
religious, and military leaders dreamed of re-creating the Roman Empire. The
first attempt began with the failed plan of Charles the Great, known as Charle-
magne, in A.D. 800. His failed effort to re-create the Holy Roman Empire was
followed by numerous attempts over the centuries by various Roman Catholic
pontiffs to fill the political and military vacuum.

Despite efforts by England's King Henry II to create a true European empire
by uniting the territories of England and France in the late 1100s, his heirs abandoned the quest after his death. Almost six centuries later, during the societal
chaos throughout Europe that followed the French Revolution, Emperor
Napoleon seized power in 1800 to pursue his plan to create an empire like

Rome. Despite numerous military victories, his opponents in Europe joined with the growing military forces of England to create an alliance that finally defeated Napoleon at Waterloo, ending his dreams of conquest.

Over a century later, the Italian dictator Benito Mussolini tried and failed to re-create the Roman Empire in the 1930s through the development of his fascist forces. At the same time, Adolf Hitler created a political, economic, and military colossus that threatened the whole world between 1939 and 1945. He dreamed that his Third Reich (literally, "Third Empire") would endure for a thousand years as a revival of the ancient glories of the Roman Empire.

THE ANTICHRIST AND THE REVIVED ROMAN EMPIRE

Daniel's ability to interpret dreams and prophetic visions brought him to the attention of Nebuchadnezzar, king of Babylon. The king had a strange dream about a great human image composed of four different metals: gold, silver, bronze, and iron. Daniel explained that this image symbolized the future course of four successive world empires, from the time of Daniel in the sixth century B.C. until the end of this age. Daniel prophesied that four major Gentile world empires would in sequence rule the known world, starting with the Babylonian Empire and proceeding through history until the time of the Second Coming of Christ. From world history we know that following the rule of Babylon would be Media-Persia, then Greece, then Rome.

In a dream Nebuchadnezzar saw a metallic image of a man that had "feet and toes, part of potters' clay, and part of iron" (Daniel 2:41). Daniel's interpretation pointed out that "the kingdom shall be divided; but there shall be in it of the strength of the iron, forasmuch as thou sawest the iron mixed with miry clay" (2:41). Later, the prophet described his own parallel vision of a beast that "had ten horns," representing the ten nations that would arise in the last days within the territory of the ancient Roman Empire (see Daniel 7:7). The two visions suggest that the fourth Gentile empire, Rome, will arise in the form of ten allied nations. Daniel's description of "ten toes" and "ten horns" may describe the future course of the European Union, which may be the embryonic power base of the coming Antichrist's world government. The prophetic time line shows that the revived Roman Empire will rise to global power about seven-plus years prior to the Second Coming of Christ.

Interpreting Nebuchadnezzar's dream, Daniel wrote:

> Thou, O king, sawest, and behold a great image. This great image, whose brightness was excellent, stood before thee; and the form thereof was terrible. This image's head was of fine gold, his breast and his arms of silver, his belly and his thighs of brass, his legs of iron, his feet part of iron and part of clay. Thou sawest till that a stone was cut out without hands, which smote the image upon his feet that were of iron and clay, and brake them to pieces. (2:31–34)

The fourth world empire, the "legs of iron," was the original Roman Empire. (That it had two legs of iron predicted the division of the empire into Eastern and Western empires.) The final portion of the manlike image was the two feet, composed of iron and clay, which represent the final stage of the revived Roman Empire in the years leading up to the battle of Armageddon. The combination of clay and iron predicted that the ten-nation alliance would include both weak and strong nations, presumably within the geographic territory of the old Roman Empire.

Later, God gave Daniel another prophetic vision that depicted the final destiny of the revived Roman Empire:

> After this I saw in the night visions, and behold a fourth beast, dreadful and terrible, and strong exceedingly; and it had great iron teeth: it devoured and brake in pieces, and stamped the residue with the feet of it: and it was diverse from all the beasts that were before it; and it had ten horns. I considered the horns, and, behold, there came up among them another little horn, before whom there were three of the first horns plucked up by the roots. (7:7–8)

This vision suggests that ten nations will join together in a Roman confederacy. Later, a dynamic new leader of Western Europe (the "little horn," symbolizing the Antichrist) will take advantage of a crisis in Europe and will seize control of three of the ten nations by military force. The remaining seven nations will then submit to the Antichrist and accept his dictatorial rule. The Antichrist's conquest of the three European nations will be his first military success on his road to supreme world power. The Antichrist will rule for an unknown number of years, but the Scriptures declare that in his position as head of the revived Roman Empire, he will guarantee a treaty, or "confirm the covenant," with Israel for a period of seven years (see Daniel 9:27). Daniel foretold the Antichrist's covenant with the revived nation of Israel in his prophecy:

> And he shall confirm the covenant with many for one week: and in the
> midst of the week he shall cause the sacrifice and the oblation to cease,
> and for the overspreading of abominations he shall make it desolate, even
> until the consummation, and that determined shall be poured upon the
> desolate. (9:27)

The Antichrist will wield absolute power over every nation on earth, as well as exercising his satanic power over the Tribulation saints who find faith in Christ during this time of brutal persecution. After the bodily resurrection (the Rapture) of the dead saints (whose spirits are now in heaven) as well as the glorification of all living Christian saints, millions of Jews and Gentiles who are left on earth will examine the Scriptures in a search for answers about why hundreds of millions of Christians have disappeared. Millions from every race will eventually reject the propaganda of the world dictator and will place their faith in God as a result of their study of the Bible and the message of the Two Witnesses and the 144,000 Jewish witnesses (see Revelation 7:14–17; 11:3–12). These converts to faith in Jesus the Messiah will come from every nation. They are the Tribulation saints described in the book of Revelation:

After this I beheld, and, lo, a great multitude, which no man could number, of all nations, and kindreds, and people, and tongues, stood before the throne, and before the Lamb, clothed with white robes, and palms in their hands.... And one of the elders answered, saying unto me, What are these which are arrayed in white robes?... And he said to me, These are they which came out of great tribulation, and have washed their robes, and made them white in the blood of the Lamb. (Revelation 7:9, 13–14)

The prophecies indicate the Antichrist's domination over the Tribulation saints will continue during the entire seven-year treaty period. The Antichrist will defile the rebuilt Temple in Jerusalem at the midpoint of the seven-year Tribulation. From that point to the time of his destruction and death in the battle of Armageddon at Jesus Christ's return will be three and a half years (see Daniel 7:25; also Revelation 13:5–7).

SIGNS OF THE ANTICHRIST'S KINGDOM

The North Atlantic Treaty Organization (NATO) was established in 1948 by the Western Allies of World War II. They created the international alliance to ensure the common defense of Western Europe against a growing military threat from the Soviet Union and the Warsaw Pact. Much has happened since the adoption of the NATO mutual-defense pact. The process of creating a European superstate began in 1957 with the Treaty of Rome and the negotiations that established the European Common Market, officially known then as the European Economic Community. The Treaty of Rome set the stage for the European Union (EU) to become an economic, political, and military colossus. In 1979, Europe held its first election for the European Parliament, creating the first directly elected, multinational superstate assembly in history.

Without realizing it, the people of Western Europe have already taken the first steps toward fulfilling Daniel's prophecy of the ten-nation superstate. The

French intellectual Jean Monnet, the spiritual father of the "United States of Europe," revealed the ultimate political objective of the new superstate: "Once a common market interest has been created, then political union will come naturally."[4] In 1992, the Treaty on European Union set the rules for a single EU currency as well as for foreign policy, security policy, and closer cooperation in justice and domestic affairs among the member nations.[5]

The EU is gradually adopting new member states, now comprising twenty-seven nations. Norway and Switzerland had declined to become members but are now reconsidering. A significant portion of the citizens of these nations see the prospect of joining the EU as a necessary evil. However, a strong minority vehemently rejects membership and openly declares that joining the EU would destroy their culture and national sovereignty.

The astonishing speed and success of the integration of the individual European economies, together with growing forces of globalization, have convinced most Europeans that national independence may be a political luxury they can no longer afford. Many of the poverty-stricken nations of Eastern Europe, including Bulgaria and Romania, have now qualified as members. They saw EU membership as a promise of economic prosperity and the only real hope to defend their weak democratic governments from communists hoping to be restored to power.[6]

THE FIRST SUPERSTATE CURRENCY

The president of Germany's powerful Bundesbank (central bank) declared that "a European currency will lead to member nations transferring their sovereignty over financial and wage policy as well as in monetary affairs."[7] Europeans are realizing that the EU could mean the practical abolishment of their historic nations, their laws, their customs, and even control over their political future. The EU's introduction of the euro currency in 1999 was a significant step toward creating the world's first superstate economy, an effective common market, and the elimination of trade barriers between member states. Euro banknotes and coins came into public circulation in 2002. The euro simplifies foreign exchange problems for corporations and governments in EU member states and thereby reduces significant currency exchange costs.

Adoption of the euro paved the way for fully integrated Europe-wide tax systems as well as a common fiscal and monetary policy. Fifteen centuries after the fall of the Roman Empire, the economically and militarily powerful nations of Europe are systematically transforming themselves into virtual provinces of the world's first superstate, the base for the coming global superstate that was described in the prophecies of Daniel and John. These developments in Europe should awaken Christians everywhere and warn us that we are entering the last days.

THE TOTALITARIANISM OF THE EUROPEAN UNION

Signs of the coming world government go far beyond a shared currency and EU trade arrangements that favor member nations over the rest of the world. Laws and regulations from the EU are already impinging on national laws, customs, and more.

British journalist Christopher Booker warned of the threat posed by the EU in a speech to the Institute of Directors, a group of major corporate directors in the United Kingdom. Booker linked the rise of international regulations in Europe to totalitarianism. The citizens of member nations, including the United Kingdom, are subject to the power of the European Union, but the European Union is not accountable to the citizenry. Booker defended his conclusion that Britain and all other EU member states are progressively surrendering their freedom, having joined an undemocratic and totalitarian society. He warned, "The illusion is still given us...that our democratically-elected politicians are still somehow in charge, able to make decisions on our behalf."[8]

However, Booker noted that "it is no longer the elected politicians who are even nominally in control. It is not even those shadowy armies of officials who, behind the scenes, at least go through the motions of formulating those decisions.... What is in control is the system itself. And, with rapidly accelerating momentum in the past few years, it has been turning into a very odd system indeed."[9]

Booker noted that useless and restrictive EU regulations were often so oppressive that when UK citizens wrote to their British member of Parliament requesting his or her intervention to solve a problem, they were given an eternal runaround involving self-justifying letters from the very EU bureaucrat who originated the offending regulation. Booker also explained that the EU system is not "in any recognizable, traditional sense a democracy. It is a perfect example of a closed system, which has not touched reality at any point.... The constituent is still in his awful mess. The only lesson he has learned, if he didn't know it already, is that the bureaucracy, the monster, is always right. Whatever it does."[10]

In a superstate system such as the European Union, unelected bureaucrats tend to continue issuing regulations without responding to criticism. In addition, the usual democratic remedy to correct bad decisions is unlikely to work because the regulators are not subject to elections or to political pressure from members of Parliament. As a result, the ability to correct bad EU decisions is virtually nonexistent.

Despite the trappings of democracy, the directly elected European Parliament cannot affect major laws, taxes, or choice of executives, but they now have the ability to at least vote on and amend two-thirds of EU laws.[11]

The pattern displayed by all international organizations is that real political power is exercised secretly by key members of an elite group, operating from behind closed and locked doors. History suggests that meaningful representative government can function only at the local or national level. Once we enter the arena of international politics, democratic government is quietly replaced by sophisticated bargaining and trade-offs negotiated behind the scenes.

The political and economic power centered in the EU's Executive Commission is but a preview of how power will be exercised in the coming world government. History suggests that a powerful individual will inevitably arise to seize political power and rule the future world government.

CHAPTER 10

FEMA, THE UN, AND NATO IN GLOBAL GOVERNMENT

Early Indicators of What the World Regime Looks Like

As we discussed in previous chapters, the government's ability to use technology to monitor every aspect of your life and mine—our financial transactions, purchases, medical treatments and diagnoses, travel, Internet searches, and more—far outweighs our ability to protect our privacy. Despite growing public concern over this loss of privacy, the governments of the United States and Canada have failed to protect citizens from government intrusion. If any branch of government, any intelligence agency, or any arm of law enforcement wants to monitor your private life and personal activities, they are free to do so. The same is true of a curious neighbor who has time on his hands and enough knowledge of where to look on the Internet to get details of your private life.

As we lose the few remaining shreds of our privacy, the government continues to create agencies and departments that intrude into our lives. A recent expansion of the shadow government that runs much of what goes on in the United States is the Federal Emergency Management Agency (FEMA). This agency potentially possesses more power during an emergency than the president or the Congress. FEMA was created to assure the political and physical survival of the federal government in the case of overwhelming natural disasters—including earthquakes, floods, and hurricanes—and attacks involving nuclear, biological, or chemical weapons.

Through FEMA, the shadow government can suspend laws and our constitutional rights by ordering the displacement of entire populations of citizens for reasons of national security. FEMA can authorize the establishment of citizen detention camps, where anyone accused of certain crimes can be held without trial for the duration of a national crisis. FEMA can also arrest and hold prisoner any suspicious citizens without an arrest warrant. Suspicious citizens can be held secretly without trial, in violation of their constitutional right to due process and the right to a fair and timely trial.

The shadow government can seize any property and can take control of food supplies and transportation systems. It can order the suspension of the Constitution by citing sufficient threats to national security, and the president has the power to declare a national emergency at any time. When that determination is announced, FEMA exercises enormous power. While the military and the Central Intelligence Agency are subject to congressional oversight, FEMA is accountable only to the president. The result is that FEMA is the most powerful government agency in the country.

EXECUTIVE ORDERS AND POTENTIAL DICTATORSHIP

FEMA was created in 1979 through Executive Order no. 12148, issued by President Jimmy Carter. The agency is designed to cooperate with the Department of Defense for future civil defense planning and coordinated efforts during national emergencies. The president has the power to suspend the Constitution in a national crisis and to turn over the reins of government to FEMA. The president can then appoint military commanders to control all state and local governments. (See information on executive orders, pages 140–41.)

Most Americans do not realize that martial law can be declared during any period of increased tension overseas or domestic economic problems, including civil unrest or an economic depression. These potentially dictatorial executive powers increased massively with the passage of the 1991 and 1994 crime bills, which increased the president's power to suspend the rights guaranteed under the Constitution. These laws also authorize the government to seize the property of those suspected of being drug dealers as well as individuals who exercise their democratic and constitutional rights to protest and demonstrate against the government.

FEMA has been enlarged through a series of executive orders signed by every successive president. While the Constitution does not refer to the existence of such a thing as a presidential executive order, these orders become federal law merely as a result of being published in the Federal Register. It is unlikely that any of the signers of the Constitution contemplated such unlimited, unexamined, and dictatorial powers to be exercised by a president. Congress is bypassed completely.

Following the terrorist attacks of September 11, 2001, President George W. Bush created the Department of Homeland Security. In 2003, FEMA was made an agency of the Department of Homeland Security. FEMA has spent only about 6 percent of its budget on emergencies arising from natural disasters such as hurricanes or earthquakes. The vast majority of its annual funding in the last decade was used to construct secret underground government-survival facilities. Such hidden and protected structures assure the continuity of the federal government in the event of a major natural disaster or a nuclear, chemical, or biological attack.[1]

A separate executive order, no. 12656, declared that the National Security Council would be the principal body directing national emergency powers. FEMA's enormous powers can be triggered by the president during any perceived domestic or foreign crisis. Sources suggest that FEMA has three hundred sophisticated mobile communications units equipped to assure government continuity and ongoing operations during a national emergency. Each mobile unit can operate independently for up to one month.[2]

Your Freedoms Held Hostage

As U.S. presidents can issue executive orders without congressional oversight or approval, a sitting president also can create laws and regulations that may eliminate your constitutional freedoms. The following executive orders were declared over the last three decades and may be enacted into law by a president's written declaration:

- No. 10990 allows the government to seize all modes of transportation and control all highways and seaports.
- No. 10995 allows the government to seize and control every portion of the communications media.
- No. 10997 makes it possible for the government to seize all electrical power, natural gas, petroleum, other fuels, plus all mineral resources— whether they are owned publicly or privately.
- No. 10998 allows the government to control all food supplies and resources, public and private, including all farms and agricultural equipment.
- No. 11000 permits the president to mobilize what could potentially include all American civilians into labor brigades under government supervision.
- No. 11002 declares that the postmaster general must create and operate a national citizen registry of every person in the country, for possible assignment to vital government service during a national emergency.
- No. 11003 allows the government to take over all airports and all aircraft.
- No. 11004 allows the Housing and Home Finance Administrator (of the agency that later became the U.S. Department of Housing and Urban Development) to relocate communities, build new housing with public funds, designate areas to be abandoned as unsafe, and establish new locations for populations.
- No. 11005 allows the government to take over railroads, inland waterways, and storage facilities—public and private.

■ No. 11921 allows the Federal Emergency Preparedness Agency to develop plans to establish presidential control over the mechanisms of production and distribution of energy sources, wages, salaries, credit, and the flow of money in U.S. financial institutions in any national emergency. Remarkably, this executive order also provides that when a state of emergency is declared by the president, Congress cannot review the action for six months.[3]

THE ARMY OF THE NEW WORLD ORDER

As your personal freedoms are being violated at home, on the international stage, plans and policies continue to advance the cause of a one-world government. On the military front, the North Atlantic Treaty Organization (NATO) is rapidly becoming the armed forces of the coming global government.

Following the end of World War II, America, the United Kingdom, and Canada supported the creation of NATO to prepare a united defensive alliance against the armies of the Soviet Union and the Warsaw Pact. NATO was founded as a defensive alliance, the most successful in history.

Meanwhile, with the ascension of the European Union and efforts to create a United States of Europe, there have been repeated negotiations to develop a united European military force separate from NATO. However, a combination of factors has prevented the plan's full implementation. European governments were reluctant to invest the necessary funds to create a world-class international military force. More important, the United States opposed an independent European military force because it could greatly reduce America's ability to enlist Europe's political, economic, and military involvement in support of America's own foreign policy goals.

However, during the last few years, Americans have grown weary of paying billions of dollars annually to provide the lion's share of the military forces necessary to protect Western Europe. Being the world's sole policeman, with the American taxpayer bearing most of the financial burden, became less and less acceptable to Washington. As a result, the United States began to pressure members of the EU to significantly increase their defense funding and to take steps toward creating a combined military force.

In 1999, following decades of failed military reorganization efforts, the European Council met in Helsinki, Finland, to plan the creation of a pan-European armed force. Composed of elite units of soldiers from each of the European Union's member nations, this rapid-reaction force initially involved sixty thousand soldiers. In the future, this force is expected to be enlarged to the point of being capable of defending Europe from any enemy force.

A political consequence of President Obama's administration and the Democratic leadership in Congress is that America plans to make severe cuts in its defense budget. The global economic crisis and its impact on the U.S. economy, together with President Obama's expensive plans to create universal healthcare, will motivate major reductions in the defense budget. The Obama administration has already spoken of cutting back on missile defenses planned to protect America and Europe. U.S. Representative Barney Frank, chairman of the House Financial Services Committee, has called for a major reduction in the military budget.

The increasing isolation of the federal government and its cuts to the defense budget will create a political-military vacuum. Following the loss of thousands of soldiers and the outlay of almost a trillion dollars in wars in Afghanistan and Iraq, the American public and its leaders will be reluctant to continue America's role as sole policeman of the world. When the United States begins to withdraw its troops from Iraq, Afghanistan, Europe, and Asia to refocus its budget and attention on American economic concerns, Europeans will come to realize they must rearm to protect their nations. A political-military power vacuum will arise as the United States focuses on its domestic problems. The vacuum may well be filled by a resurgent European superpower under the leadership of the coming Antichrist.

If America follows through on plans to reduce its military support for Europe, that will likely motivate the EU member nations to increase their military budgets and their armed forces.

NATO's New Imperialism

Representatives of the twenty-six member states of NATO met in 1999 to negotiate the basis for the expansion of the alliance in the new millennium. The most serious issue involved the role of NATO military forces in future conflicts outside Europe. Prior to the Kosovo conflict, for example, NATO had refused to become involved in military operations outside the geographic region of its member states. The proximity of Kosovo to NATO's member states in Western Europe and its location between the NATO member states of Greece and Hungary provided some justification for a military intervention beyond NATO's territory.

Though some members of NATO, including Britain, Canada, Italy, and Turkey, contributed significantly to the 1991 Gulf War to repel Iraq's invasion of Kuwait, they did so as individual nations allied with the United States and not under the terms of their treaty with NATO. However, the precedent-setting NATO summit of 1999 resulted in a transformation of the role and purpose of the alliance. The summit produced a document announcing that NATO is no longer bound to the principle of providing only a defensive alliance for its member states. The new strategic concept for the alliance is a complete reversal of that defensive stance. This change in military doctrine will set the stage for the coming world government.

I am indebted to Joe de Courcy, editor of *Intelligence Digest,* the most important private intelligence analysis company in the world, for alerting me to the political significance of NATO's shift in strategic doctrine. This new strategic doctrine began by declaring that NATO's "essential and enduring purpose…is to safeguard the freedom and security of all its members by political and military means."[4] While this language appears innocent, the phrase "by political and military means" opened the door for NATO to move into geographic territories and activities far beyond its traditional role of military defense. The word "political" creates a justification for surveillance, espionage, political pressure, and many other unprecedented activities.

NATO's Strategic Doctrine

The 1999 document defines the strategic doctrine that will govern future military or political intervention by NATO:

> The security of the Alliance remains subject to a wide variety of military *and non-military risks*.... These risks include uncertainty and instability in and around the Euro-Atlantic area and the possibility of regional crises at the periphery of the Alliance which could evolve rapidly. Some countries in and around the Euro-Atlantic area face serious economic, social and political difficulties. Ethnic and religious rivalries, territorial disputes, inadequate or failed efforts at reform, the abuse of human rights, and the dissolution of states can lead to local and even regional instability. The resulting tensions could lead to crises affecting Euro-Atlantic stability, to human suffering, and to armed conflicts. Such conflicts could affect the security of the Alliance by spilling over into neighboring countries, including NATO countries, or in other ways, and could also affect the security of other states.[5] (emphasis added)

This definition of military "and non-military" situations that could provoke military intervention is astonishing. NATO, in its first fifty years, refused to intervene militarily unless a member nation's territory was attacked. Now the alliance holds that "uncertainty and instability in and around the Euro-Atlantic area" or even "at the periphery of the Alliance" could justify military intervention. Situations that could provoke a NATO military intervention include "ethnic and religious rivalries," "abuse of human rights," and "local and even regional instability."

The NATO doctrine justifies its right to intervene militarily or politically in virtually any surrounding nation or territory. This policy reminds me of the imperialism of previous centuries, whereby superpowers such as Spain, Great Britain, and France justified military intervention in any part of the world that they arbitrarily declared to be within their "sphere of influence."

Incredibly, the strategic concept provides a specific rationale for NATO to justify a future invasion of another nation:

Alliance security interests can be affected by *other risks of a wider nature,* including acts of terrorism, sabotage and organized crime, and by the disruption of the flow of vital resources. The uncontrolled movement of large numbers of people, particularly as a consequence of armed conflicts, can also pose problems for security and stability affecting the Alliance.[6] (emphasis added)

The nations of the Western alliance believe they have the right to invade or intervene in any other nation because of NATO's belief regarding the existence in that country of "acts of terrorism, sabotage and organized crime, and by the disruption of the flow of vital resources." NATO declares a further justification for military intervention: the attempt by a nation within NATO's declared security zone to acquire nuclear, biological, and chemical weapons and the development of the means to deliver such weapons that "can pose a direct military threat to the Allies' populations, territory and forces."[7]

The stated justifications for a potential NATO invasion of another country are so varied and vague that virtually any pretext may satisfy the rationale. Gen. Klaus Naumann, former chairman of the alliance's military committee (now retired), defined the geographical regions that NATO considered to be within its enlarged security zone. The zone included "the nations resting on its [NATO's] periphery from Morocco to the Indian Ocean." In other words, NATO is willing to intervene militarily from North Africa throughout the Middle East, including the Arabian Peninsula, and extending as far east as Iran. NATO soldiers have been fighting Muslim insurgents in Afghanistan under the authorization of the UN Security Council.

The NATO document also refers to the enormous effort to integrate military structures, weapons, and tactics of new alliance members to "prevent the re-nationalization of defence policies." Key elements of this strategy include:

Collective force planning; common funding; common operational
planning; multinational formations, headquarters and command
arrangements; an integrated air defence system; a balance of roles and
responsibilities among the Allies; the stationing and deployment of
forces outside home territory when required; arrangements, including
planning, for crisis management and reinforcement; common standards
and procedures for equipment, training and logistics; joint and combined doctrines and exercises when appropriate; and infrastructure,
armaments and logistics cooperation.[8]

Throughout history, whenever an aggressive military alliance or power has
arisen to threaten the sovereignty and integrity of neighbor states, the surrounding nations have formed their own military alliances. These developments
could create the preconditions for the fulfillment of John's prophecy in Revelation about the rise of the Antichrist, whose power initially will be based on ten
nations within the former territory of the Roman Empire.

The Question of a UN Army

It is possible to imagine NATO forces being used to achieve the United Nation's
globalist goals. In the future, NATO's military strength and advanced technology could be employed to support the United Nation's secret mission, which is
to achieve a world government.

The creation of an effective international military force is a key goal of the
globalists. Only a permanent standing army of significant size would provide
the UN Security Council the power to enforce the will of the world body
against the military forces of an individual nation or group of nations.

The number of military and civilian personnel involved in UN peacekeeping operations tripled between 2000 and 2009. The UN Security Council
deployed troops in two dozen nations at a cost of more than eight billion dollars in 2008.[9] In early 2009, eighteen UN peacekeeping operations were under
way in Africa, Asia, Europe, Haiti, and the Middle East.

UN FAILURES VERSUS NATO'S GAIN?

During the 1990s and the first eight years of the new millennium, the United Nations engaged in more peacekeeping operations than in its first five decades. And more often than not, UN peacekeeping operations were and are military disasters. During the Rwandan civil war, a group of Belgian UN troops was massacred by African rebels without any UN military retaliation. In 2000, UN troops were massacred in Sierra Leone without any reprisal. At the time of horrific national disasters in Somalia and Rwanda, the United Nations repeatedly tried but failed to create a professional international army from disparate units of dozens of small military forces. Often the donated ammunition was of a different caliber than the weapons, the troops were not trained to use the communications equipment that was supplied, and soldiers were often commanded by foreign officers unable to speak their language. As a result, there has been little or no improvement in the world body's military capabilities.

The repeated failure of the United Nations to effectively put troops on the ground in various trouble spots has given rise to calls for a permanent standing UN military force. One study of the 1994 Rwandan tragedy revealed that the United Nations saw disaster coming but was paralyzed by competing political agendas and the indifference of the UN Security Council. When the United Nations finally acted, after horrible pictures of Rwandan genocide filled television screens around the world, it was a case of too little, too late.

Considering the horrendous failures of UN peacekeeping missions in Somalia, Rwanda, and Sierra Leone, it is possible the United Nations could seek an ongoing military agreement with NATO. Contrast UN peacekeeping mission failures with NATO's successful military campaigns during the 1991 Gulf War, the 1998–99 Kosovo bombing campaign, and NATO's Afghanistan mission since 2003. A much faster and more expedient way for the United Nations to achieve the military effectiveness required to enforce the will of the UN Security Council would be to utilize NATO's unified, integrated military forces.

THE GLOBALIST THREAT TO NATIONAL SOVEREIGNTY

During UN Security Council debates regarding NATO's 1999 Kosovo intervention, concerns were raised that NATO's action represented a dangerous precedent and a threat to the sovereignty of every nation outside the NATO alliance. Russia, China, India, and many third world nations issued statements denouncing NATO's justification of its Kosovo intervention. A thoughtful article published in the *Jordan Times* stated:

> But the most important issue raised by the NATO Yugoslavia Confrontation is the inviolability of a country's sovereignty, or more specifically under what circumstances is intervention in an independent state's internal affairs permissible and who should be allowed to intervene. Many of the states opposing the NATO action fear it will set a precedent of support for separatist movements which could be used against China in Tibet, against Russia in Chechnya, and against India in Kashmir. Another concern is the bypassing of the UN by NATO. NATO is viewed as simply promoting US interests and in effect making the US a sort of world policeman.[10]

Jordan is friendly to the interests of the West. But if Jordan expressed such deep concerns about the threat to all other nations' sovereignty from NATO's imperialistic policies, you can imagine the concern of anti-Western nations. Russia, China, India, Syria, Iran, Venezuela, and Cuba have strong reasons to fear what they perceive as a new wave of imperialism from the NATO powers.

ENLARGING THE UNITED NATIONS' POWERS

While UN spokesmen are usually quite discreet in discussing the approaching world government, occasionally a report or a diplomat's speech will reveal the real agenda. Former British foreign secretary Douglas Hurd stated in an interview that the United Nations needs to prepare itself to take on an "imperial role." He declared that the United Nations must usurp national sovereignty and take control of countries as the occupying military and political power when governments collapse, as in Kosovo, Somalia, Rwanda, and Sierra Leone. During an interview, Hurd drew attention to what he called "a new phase in the world's history." He cited a need for the United Nations to intervene much earlier in crisis situations to "prevent things getting to the stage where countries are run by corrupt war lords, as in Somalia." Hurd warned that since the breakup of the former Soviet Union, the United States was the lone superpower but it had no wish to become the "policeman of the world."[11]

More and more, European and North American politicians are encouraging this new variation of neocolonialism. Some propose that the United Nations establish a new type of trusteeship over "failed states," nations whose governments are collapsing due to drought, famine, corruption, or civil war. Examples in recent years include Somalia, the Congo, Rwanda, and Haiti. Tragic situations in Africa, as displayed daily on television, provide ready-made propaganda for those who have an underlying goal to establish the United Nations as the nucleus for a world government.

ISRAEL'S STRATEGIC PLACE IN THE WORLD

The nation of Israel occupies a strategic location on the land bridge that links Europe, Asia, and Africa. The geography of this tiny nation makes it a focus of the rest of the world, from superpowers to the Arab nations that surround it. The nation that wields the military power controlling the land bridge between the three continents is in a position to dominate world events.

Due to the strength of its army and air force, Israel can militarily dominate the eastern Mediterranean and the surrounding nations of the Middle East. However, a major war between Israel and its enemies would almost certainly exceed the devastation of any regional war waged since Israel's rebirth in 1948. Seven of the largest arms-importing nations in the world are found in the Middle East, surrounding the nation of Israel.[12]

International organizations, including the United Nations, continue to pass resolutions against Israel. Twenty-five centuries ago the prophet Zechariah foretold that the nations of the world would form a military alliance to attack Jerusalem and Israel in the last days.

> Behold, I will make Jerusalem a cup of trembling unto all the people round about, when they shall be in the siege both against Judah and against Jerusalem.
>
> And in that day will I make Jerusalem a burdensome stone for all people: all that burden themselves with it shall be cut in pieces, though all the people of the earth be gathered against it. (12:2–3)

THE FUTURE OF A ONE-WORLD GOVERNMENT

Our generation faces the greatest crisis in history. One road leads toward unimaginable destruction, of the sort prophesied by Zechariah, that could mean the end of civilization. Our world is endangered by Islamic terrorism, rampant nationalism, and age-old ethnic hatreds. Rogue nations and terror groups will soon use the devastating power of nuclear, chemical, biological, and electromagnetic weapons. These threats could lead to catastrophic horrors exceeding the worst devastation of World War II.

Another road leads toward the New World Order, a global totalitarian government that would seek to extinguish human freedom. A century ago the British statesman Lord Acton warned, "Absolute power corrupts absolutely." A strong argument can be made that human freedom and democratic choice can prevail only in a political system that permanently distributes power among different groups to create checks and balances. However, current trends lead inexorably toward a New World Order in which all political, military, and religious power will be consolidated. Total control will be exercised by one supranational global institution led by one supreme leader, the Antichrist.

Even if the first few leaders of the New World Order are democratic in their intentions, eventually a leader will rise to power with a thoroughly evil agenda. According to the biblical prophecies, the Antichrist will achieve absolute political power over the global government, enabling him to create a worldwide dictatorship. When a global government rules, there will be no independent nation-states left to mount military or political resistance.

Daniel and John foretold thousands of years ago that an extremely powerful military, economic, and political power will arise in the last days, an extraordinary revival of the ancient Roman Empire. The revived Roman Empire will use peace treaties and wars to ultimately encompass the nations of the world during the seven-year Tribulation (see Daniel 9 and Revelation 13). However, Daniel prophesied that the nations of the East will rebel against the empire's global domination.

John declared, "And the sixth angel poured out his vial upon the great river Euphrates; and the water thereof was dried up, that the way of the kings of the east might be prepared" (Revelation 16:12). The nations of the East will mobilize their forces with an army numbering two hundred million men (see Revelation 9:16). This unprecedented army will wage war against the Western nations under the military leadership of the Antichrist.

The imperialistic political and military developments within NATO and the defensive response of nations such as Russia, China, and India are setting the stage for the last-days events described in the Scriptures. The prophecies of the Word of God provide the only hope for humanity as it is subjugated by totalitarian political, military, and police powers. When it seems there is no hope left for human freedom, Scripture assures us that Jesus Christ will return from heaven with His army of angels and the resurrected saints of the Church. Christ will utterly defeat the Antichrist and his evil forces forever.

Following the defeat of the Antichrist, Christ will establish His eternal Kingdom on earth. Under Christ's rule as King, humanity will finally experience freedom, justice, and righteous government for the first time since the Garden of Eden.

CHAPTER 11

THE MARK OF THE BEAST— POPULATION TRACKING

With Microchips, It's Easy to Give Every Person a Number

Our loss of privacy, rights, and freedoms is of concern on two levels. The first, of course, is that democratic societies are founded on the principle of rule by the people, the rights of individuals, and the requirement that government be accountable to the citizens. The globalist elite are doing everything they can to overturn these foundations of democracy.

But there is a second, more important reason that we need to be concerned about the move toward a centralized global government. Students of prophecy know that such a move is not merely the work of idealistic leaders who are misled about the best way to prevent future world wars. The push for a one-world government is an early development that sets the stage for global rule by the Antichrist. In addition, accelerated technological developments in the surveillance and tracking of individuals, and the pervasive governmental invasion of our lives, reveals many of the tools that could be used by the Antichrist's regime.

The Antichrist's totalitarian police control leading to Armageddon will involve "the mark, or the name of the beast, or the number of his name" (Revelation 13:17). These three identifying marks will be used—either simultaneously or separately—to identify the followers of the Antichrist and those who indicate they are willing to worship him as "god." The mark will be required for anyone to conduct business, make purchases, and acquire food and other necessities—in other words, to survive on earth. Those who reject the Antichrist's false claim to be god by rejecting the mark will either flee to the hills or will be martyred. Those who remain faithful to the One True God will refuse the Mark of the Beast.

The mark itself will be applied to the right hand or forehead of any adult who worships the Antichrist. The mark would be applied to the forehead for a variety of reasons, including that many individuals don't have a right hand due to an accident or congenital condition. It is also possible that the location of the mark—either right hand or forehead—could designate the person's relative status as a follower of the Antichrist.

The Bible mentions the Mark of the Beast, his name, and the number of his name, which is 666. The mark is different from but related to the name and also differs from the number 666. In John's prophecy recorded in Revelation 13:16–18, we are not told the exact nature of the mark. It might be a physical brand visible on the surface of the skin, including either the actual name of the Antichrist or the number 666.

However, using existing technology, the mark or number 666 can be implanted under the skin of every person using an RFID (radio frequency identification) microchip. A powerful electronic scanner could detect the chip from a distance and reveal all your personal information, far more than your name, address, age, and marital status. While the implanted microchip and its information would be readable by a radio frequency scanner, a person would not know when or where his private information was being accessed—or who was accessing the information.

THE NATURE OF THE NAME OF THE BEAST

It is possible that the Antichrist might change the name that was given to him at birth to a new name that will become the "name of the beast." The Scriptures record that God changed the name of many characters in the Bible at a key moment of crisis in their lives. The new name reflected the person's new spiritual condition. Abram was changed to Abraham, Jacob to Israel, and Saul to Paul. Because names can change, and because the Bible remains silent on the matter, it is futile to speculate about the name or identity of the future Antichrist. Where God has drawn a veil over a significant matter, it is spiritual arrogance for a Christian to attempt to reveal it. Those who live through the terrible trials of the Great Tribulation will recognize the Antichrist based on his fulfillment of the Bible's prophecies, especially when he signs a seven-year treaty with Israel (see Daniel 9:24–27), regardless of what name he goes by.

It is inevitable that many Greek and Hebrew names will, by random chance, be equivalent to the numeric value 666. While studying my library of books on prophecy, archaeology, and theology, I once compiled a list of more than eighty-five different individuals who over the centuries have been identified as the Antichrist. Some have speculated that the Antichrist will be a reincarnated evil leader from the past, such as Nimrod, King Ahab, Judas Iscariot, Julius Caesar, Nero, Vespasian, Titus, or Hadrian.

In recent centuries, prophetic speculators have identified numerous potential Antichrist candidates, including Napoleon, a variety of powerful popes, Kaiser Wilhelm II (emperor of Germany until 1918), Adolf Hitler, Benito Mussolini, Henry Kissinger, Jimmy Carter, Ronald Reagan, George H. W. Bush, Bill Clinton, George W. Bush, Mikhail Gorbachev, Mao Zedong, King Juan Carlos of Spain, the Hapsburgs (a family of Holy Roman emperors and other royal rulers), Saddam Hussein, and David Rockefeller. Obviously, these prophetic speculations proved to be incorrect. Attempting to identify the Antichrist before he appears is as futile as trying to pick the date for the Rapture. The 666 identification of the Antichrist's name will be relevant only for the Tribulation believers who are alive during the seven-year Tribulation period. The prophetic revelation regarding 666 will warn those living during the terrible time of persecution to reject the Mark of the Beast. Because they follow Christ, they will be aware of God's warning to reject the Antichrist at all costs, even the cost of their lives. The Scripture warns that anyone who takes the Mark of the Beast (accepting him as god) will be condemned to the lake of fire (see Revelation 14:9–11).

TECHNOLOGY SETS THE STAGE
FOR THE MARK OF THE BEAST

Automated-teller machines, RFID chips beneath the skin, and laser scanning technology illustrate the ease with which every person on earth could be located and identified, at anytime, anyplace. Scanning devices, including high-speed, long-distance optical readers and iris scanners, as well as radio-frequency ID scanners, are used at government buildings, universities, industrial plants, airports, and border stations to read your identity or the license plate of your car from hundreds of yards away.

New technology is making it feasible for RFID microchips to be painlessly implanted beneath the skin. A person can use the subcutaneous chip to complete secure financial transactions or communicate wirelessly with a computer or other digital device. But having had the chip implanted, the person also can be identified and tracked continuously. Kevin Warwick, professor of cybernetics at Reading University in England, claimed to be the first person in the world to be voluntarily implanted. Warwick experimented on himself by implanting a sophisticated computer chip that enabled him to transmit signals to the university's communications system. The implanted device was twenty-three millimeters long and three millimeters wide and emitted its unique signal only in the presence of radio frequency waves from transmitters in an intelligent building.

An enlarged image of RFID chips that are small enough to be implanted beneath the skin of humans or animals

"The potential for this technology is enormous. It is quite possible for an implant to replace an Access or Visa card," Warwick stated. "Individuals with implants could be clocked in and out of their business automatically." Despite their commercial advantages, the professor warns, "An individual might not even be able to visit the toilet without a machine knowing about it."[1]

Your Exact Location Is Known

New surveillance technologies are rapidly creating a permanent surveillance society controlled by the shadow government. Unseen watchers can track your location and activities twenty-four hours a day. The new totalitarian surveillance systems exceed anything conceived by the Nazi Gestapo or the Russian KGB.

A development known as Digital Angel involves implanting a combination RFID and GPS microchip beneath the skin of an employee. The chip identifies the person and instantly locates him or her (within a distance of three feet) anywhere on the planet through the Global Positioning System. With Digital Angel, it is known when an employee enters the building, greets the receptionist, gets a cup of coffee, makes photocopies, works at his or her desk, or uses the rest room. It is known when the person leaves for lunch and when he or she returns. It is known how much time the person spends in meetings or walking the halls or visiting a colleague. This is a new and very precise way to keep employees under a microscope.

Applied Digital Solutions in Louisville, Kentucky, patented the Digital Angel device as a "personal tracking and recovery system" to assist in locating missing children, mentally challenged patients, and prisoners in house-arrest programs. It can also monitor the heart rate and other vital data of medical patients while they are away from a hospital.[2]

A company spokesperson says Digital Angel can also track lost hikers and persons who have been abducted, including "military, diplomatic, and other essential government personnel."[3] When implanted beneath the skin, the transceiver is powered electromechanically through the movement of nearby muscles. The device can also be powered with microbatteries when it is being used to keep track of objects such as rare paintings and other valuable items. The company is looking for further applications in the areas of law enforcement, medical programs, intelligence agencies, and security. However, Marc Rotenberg, director of the Electronic Privacy Information Center in Washington DC, warned of the dangers to our privacy and freedom from such Big Brother technology: "It sounds dreadful. That's about as bad as it gets."[4]

THE NATURE AND USE OF THE MARK OF THE BEAST

And he causeth all, both small and great, rich and poor, free and bond, to receive a mark in their right hand, or in their foreheads: and that no man might buy or sell, save he that had the mark, or the name of the beast, or the number of his name. Here is wisdom. Let him that hath understanding count the number of the beast: for it is the number of a man; and his number is Six hundred threescore and six. (Revelation 13:16–18)

There is something both deeply mysterious and fascinating about the Mark of the Beast. The mark will be a physical, and perhaps visible, mark that the False Prophet will demand that every man and woman receive on their right hand or forehead. Bearing the mark will indicate that the individual willingly worships the Beast, who is the coming global dictator, the satanic Antichrist. If someone does not possess the mark, that person will not be able to "buy or sell" during the Great Tribulation. The universal application of this monetary control system was impossible until the end of the twentieth century. However, the introduction of laser scans, iris scans, implantable RFID chips, and computerized financial systems now makes the Mark of the Beast system completely feasible. All the necessary technology now exists.

The introduction of this diabolical system will place humanity in an invisible but completely controlled economic prison. The global economic and political system of the last days will be under the absolute control of the Antichrist and his partner, the False Prophet. The mark 666 will enforce the worldwide worship of the Antichrist. During the final three and a half years leading up to the battle of Armageddon, the Antichrist and False Prophet will rule the world with the supernatural power of Satan. This will be far worse than any other tyranny in human history, even worse than the horrors of the Nazis during the Holocaust. During the Holocaust there were nations that would provide sanctuary to escaping Jews and others targeted by the Nazis. However, in the last days the Antichrist will control *every* nation. There will be no other country offering refuge.

And consider that even within a totalitarian nation, it is sometimes possible to bribe a police officer or border guard with gold or to buy food with silver if you don't have the national currency. However, the Mark of the Beast system will probably eliminate money in the form of paper currency, coin, and paper documents such as certificates of deposit or Treasury bills. It will force all people to buy and sell solely through a system that will require the possession of their own, individual 666 mark. Without it, people won't find employment, won't be able to earn an income, and won't be allowed to conduct business, complete any financial transaction, or purchase daily necessities.

Efforts to Protect the Money Supply

Coins and especially currency have presented a problem to national governments for a long time. The U.S. Treasury Department and the Secret Service wage a continuous war against domestic and foreign counterfeiters. According to the National Research Council, billions of dollars in counterfeit U.S. currency are produced annually by high-tech computer printers and copiers. Every year, for example, Iran counterfeits tens of billions of U.S. dollars in currency. Recent reports claim Iran can even produce "superbills," bills of exceptionally high quality that are virtually indistinguishable from genuine currency.[5]

A line of Canon color copiers is astonishing in its ability to reproduce U.S. currency. In an attempt to eliminate the illegal use of sophisticated copiers, Canon introduced several innovative technologies. One technique involves a sensor in the copier that recognizes a currency image and refuses to copy it. In addition, new Canon copiers encode an almost invisible identification number in all images produced by each individual copier. This enables agents of the U.S. Secret Service to examine a counterfeit bill and determine the serial number of the copy machine that produced it. The copier can then be tracked to the original purchaser.

On another front in the counterfeit war, the U.S. Treasury plans to add a hidden bar code to new currency. The code would be nearly invisible within an intricate design on the bill. Another technique is to introduce in the currency design moiré-inducing patterns that produce distortions when scanning equipment or a photocopier tries to replicate the bill's design. The Treasury uses microprint only six thousandths of an inch wide, which is virtually impossible to see or to duplicate.

With the rise of the euro in the European Union, the European Central Bank is concerned about the staggering increase in counterfeiting. As a result the bank began embedding RFID tags into the fibers of the special paper used in euro banknotes.[6] The U.S. Treasury Department uses magnetic inks that allow sensors in money-counting devices and vending machines to verify whether bills are real. Both the United States and Britain have introduced in their larger-denomination bills magnetic security threads that can be detected by airport security scanners, which would alert authorities if a large quantity of such bills is being transported into the nation. Red and blue microfibers found in the new U.S. currency can be detected by special airport scanners even if the money is concealed in luggage.

In addition, the United States and the United Kingdom use watermarks and colored fibers that respond to ultraviolet or infrared light, which allow bank scanning machines to detect and verify the bills. Special color-shifting inks that change color when you tilt the viewing angle have already been introduced in higher-denomination bills. The Canadian mint introduced tiny square holograms created from thin layers of ceramic molecules that shift from gold to green depending on the viewing angle. This hologram will not reproduce on color copiers.

Plans to Replace U.S. Currency

Both governments and banks would love to eliminate all coins and paper currency by replacing money with electronic-funds transfers. The embedding of RFID chips in billions of consumer products will soon make it possible to eliminate cash. John's prophecy in Revelation 13 looks ahead to the generation that will be living during the last days, when the Antichrist's global government could possibly eliminate cash. People will be able to "buy or sell" only if they worship the Antichrist, showing that his regime will control the world's economy.

Doing away with paper currency and coins would make many criminal activities much more difficult to finance. Tax evasion, money laundering, drug dealing, and numerous other criminal and terrorist activities would be much more challenging to finance and implement in a cashless society. Banks hate cash because it is cumbersome. Cash must constantly be transferred to and from the U.S. Mint, the Federal Reserve banks, and thousands of banks throughout America. Already, the vast majority of financial transactions take place with no physical money changing hands. Most of the world's money no longer exists in the form of currency or coins.

The largest international banking system in the world, the Society for Worldwide Interbank Financial Telecommunication (SWIFT), has a sophisticated financial system that allows companies and individuals to transfer large amounts of money worldwide in only seconds. SWIFT handles 90 percent of the world's international monetary transfers between virtually all major banking institutions. As of February 2009, SWIFT linked 8,896 financial institutions in 209 countries.[7] More than six trillion dollars is transferred across international borders in some fifteen million financial transactions every twenty-four hours. The European Union strongly supports efforts to streamline international financial transfer payments as a vital step on the path to a global superstate.

A GLOBAL ECONOMIC COLLAPSE

No one can accurately predict when a government will "hit the wall" financially. That final moment of crisis will occur when the national debt and its compounding interest charges rise so high that combined national tax revenues are unable to cover the interest payments. At some point Western governments will fail to qualify for additional credit. They will be unable to borrow international funds because the Chinese Central Bank, the Middle Eastern Arab sovereign funds, Taiwan, South Korea, and other foreign lenders will realize that they will never be repaid, except in grossly inflated and thus massively devalued currency.

Numerous third world countries have reached this point in the past and have declared a moratorium on their debts. And now, after decades of growing deficits worldwide and, more recently, President Obama's trillions allocated in the 2009 stimulus plan, governments will be forced to admit they are going broke. This will be true not only in North America but also in the EU countries.

Like a consumer whose income cannot sustain his lifestyle, a nation cannot continue to borrow forever. Finally bankruptcy, economic collapse, and hyper-inflation are the only remaining options. The U.S. government has the ability to create more money using a variety of methods, from printing more currency to the various methods recently used by the Bush and Obama administrations, including trillion-dollar-plus bailout stimulus packages. These steps only delay the ultimate devastation of the housing and credit markets and other financial crises and postpone the economic collapse. Since the government can print money, the temptation is overwhelming to inflate the currency to allow the federal government to continue paying its bills. Using hyperinflation, the government, in effect, gradually repudiates its national debt by repaying bondholders with devalued currency.

When American financial markets crumble, global financial markets and the world economy will be wiped out. The staggering size of the debt now held by U.S. corporate and government bond markets is extremely dangerous. However, the speculative bond and stock markets are paragons of conservative strength in comparison to the monstrous American financial derivatives market. Financial derivative markets are highly speculative contracts that make a bet on the future value of any number of financial instruments, such as the value of the U.S. dollar in comparison to a basket of international currencies (euro, yen, pound). These contracts involve massive leverage, meaning that a drop of 1 percent in a currency's value could be magnified (with leverage) to a loss/gain of 100 percent of an investment.

Beyond the unbelievable loss/gain generated in the derivatives markets, there is very little official market oversight or regulation. In contrast, the U.S. and international stock markets, bond markets, and commodities markets are under surveillance by various financial regulators. There are thousands of applicable laws, regulations, and reporting requirements, as well as extensive government oversight. However, though the size of the financial derivatives markets dwarfs the much smaller stock, bond, and commodity markets, there are virtually no stringent reporting requirements, almost no rules or regulations, and very little governmental oversight. It is therefore no surprise that a large part of the global financial and economic crisis currently facing the world was triggered by staggering losses in the various derivatives markets by banks, investment houses, and extremely wealthy individuals.

Here is just one example. The total notional amount (the face-value amount used to calculate payments on that instrument) of all the outstanding financial risks or positions at the end of June 2004 stood at $53 trillion. The staggering size of the very speculative U.S. financial derivatives market grew, by March 2008, to $81 trillion.[8] Meanwhile, the amount of money at risk in the worldwide financial derivatives market exceeded $596 trillion, according to the Bank for International Settlements.[9] Aside from the inherent risk involved in such an enormous amount of funds invested in just one extremely high-risk area, the real danger arises from the fact that these little-understood, highly leveraged financial derivatives investments are unregulated and unreported by any stock exchange or government regulators. Banks, brokerage houses, and insurance companies created hundreds of sophisticated financial derivatives contracts that never existed before, and they issued them without any rules to limit the risk. Unlike the known procedures involved in conventional stocks and bonds, many experienced investors and financial brokers do not fully understand how the complicated derivatives contracts are supposed to work. Subprime mortgage contracts are only a small portion of these dangerous derivatives market instruments where high-risk mortgages were bundled and sold to innocent investors who did not understand the underlying risks.

The inevitable inflation that will follow the trillions of dollars spent on stimulus packages will rob citizens of their savings while making rational economic-investment decisions virtually impossible. Inflation punishes citizens who are savers, such as holders of long-term bonds, while it favors governments and individuals who borrow money, because they will repay their loans using much cheaper dollars. Obviously, the greatest benefit will be felt by the biggest debtor of all, the U.S. government.

History reveals that inflation is the government's favorite method to repudiate its debts. Years ago economist John Maynard Keynes wrote, "Lenin is said to have declared that the best way to destroy the capitalist system was to debauch the currency. By a continuing process of inflation governments can confiscate, secretly and unobserved, an important part of the wealth of their citizens."[10]

This incredibly dangerous financial derivatives market could certainly be the trigger for the coming financial collapse that the Bible indicates will occur in the last days leading to the rise of Antichrist and the revived Roman Empire.

Robert Mundell is known in Europe as the "father of the euro," the world's first transnational currency. Mundell has been lecturing for years on the urgent need for the creation of a new international currency to be known as the DEY, which would be a combination of the U.S. dollar, the euro, and the Japanese yen. Mundell openly proclaimed that only *a global economic crisis* would create the opportunity for a global currency. He stated, " 'International monetary reform usually becomes possible only in response to a felt need and the threat of a global crisis.' This Nobel Prize winner also pointed his finger to the possible trigger event, saying that the 'global crisis would have to involve the dollar,' and that a world currency should be viewed as 'a contingency' to a global dollar disaster."[11]

THE ANTICHRIST, THE NUMBER 666, AND THE MARK OF THE BEAST

For two thousand years the number 666 has been particularly ominous, especially in the minds of Christians, and has formed the basis of countless speculations. A Russian news article revealed that many members and priests of the

Russian Orthodox Church protested participation in their government's introduction of a tax identification number for each citizen. The ID numbers are
rendered as bar codes on tax ID application forms and are scanned by bar code
readers. Some Russians believe the three sets of parallel lines in each bar code
stand for the number six and suggest that the bar code is tied into the 666
Mark of the Beast. They fear the bar code numbers, which automatically
include three sixes, will someday replace their Christian names in Russia's computer databases.[12]

> Here is wisdom. Let him that hath understanding count the number of
> the beast: for it is the number of a man; and his number is Six hundred
> threescore and six. (Revelation 13:18)

The prophet John instructs the reader who has spiritual and biblical "understanding [to] count the number of the beast." Over the centuries a number of
serious students of the Bible have attempted to "count the number" to discern
the true meaning of this mysterious number. The apostle John wrote the book
of Revelation in approximately A.D. 96 in Greek, the language commonly used
in the eastern provinces of the Roman world.

A curious feature of Greek and Hebrew is that they do not use separate symbols for each of the numerical digits (1, 2, 3). Instead, each letter of the Greek
and Hebrew alphabets serves a dual purpose, standing as both a letter and a
number. This is somewhat similar to the more limited alphanumeric system
of Roman numerals where X stood for ten, C for one hundred, and M for one
thousand. However, the Greeks used every letter of the alphabet to express a
number. To illustrate, imagine that the letter A stands for the number 1, the letter B stands for 2, and so forth through the entire alphabet. Thus, when John
recorded the number of the Beast in Revelation 13:18, he wrote it in the original Greek manuscript using the three Greek letters that represent the numbers
600 and 60 and 6. The three letters having these numerical values (600, 60, 6 =
666) were translated in the English King James Version of the New Testament as
"Six hundred threescore and six."

This number in Revelation 13:18 does not allow us to speculate in advance regarding the name of the future Antichrist. Rather, once the Antichrist is revealed, Bible believers will compare his name to the Greek number 666 and confirm that he is the Antichrist. There is a slim possibility that his name will equal 666 in the Hebrew language as well. The numeric system is not applicable in any other language, so it is useless to consider names rendered in English or other languages.

CONSEQUENCES OF RECEIVING THE MARK OF THE BEAST

And I heard a great voice out of the temple saying to the seven angels, Go your ways, and pour out the vials of the wrath of God upon the earth. And the first went, and poured out his vial upon the earth; and there fell a noisome and grievous sore upon the men which had the mark of the beast, and upon them which worshipped his image. (Revelation 16:1–2)

God hates Satan's 666 "mark of the beast" because the Lord created humans to live in spiritual harmony with Him, not with Satan and his ultimate evil representative, the Antichrist. If anyone willingly (even under coercion of the threat of death) accepts the Antichrist's mark, his or her soul will be lost forever.

During the Tribulation, horrible skin infections will break out on those who accept the mark (see Revelation 16:1–2). Perhaps the sores are physically related to the technique used to put the mark or the number 666 on a person's forehead or right hand. More likely, the sores will be the result of the supernatural judgment of God.

And the third angel followed them, saying with a loud voice, If any man worship the beast and his image, and receive his mark in his forehead, or in his hand, the same shall drink of the wine of the wrath of God, which is poured out without mixture into the cup of his indignation; and he shall be tormented with fire and brimstone in the presence of the holy angels, and in the presence of the Lamb: And the smoke of their torment ascendeth up for ever and ever: and they have no rest day nor night, who worship the beast and his image, and whosoever receiveth the mark of his name. (Revelation 14:9–11)

In addition to the terrible earthly consequences, the worst punishment will follow the death of those who choose to worship the Antichrist. The eternal wrath of God will be poured out on all who reject Jesus Christ and willingly worship Satan and his Antichrist as their "god."

THE VICTORY OF THE MARTYRS

It will take tremendous faith and courage for Tribulation saints to reject the 666 mark when they know it will mean their beheading and probably the beheading of the members of their families also. However, the brave saints of the Tribulation period are promised an honored position in God's Millennial Kingdom on earth.

God's promise is clear:

And I saw thrones, and they sat upon them, and judgment was given unto them: and I saw the souls of them that were beheaded for the witness of Jesus, and for the word of God, and which had not worshipped the beast, neither his image, neither had received his mark upon their foreheads, or in their hands; and they lived and reigned with Christ a thousand years. (Revelation 20:4)

The choice to be made in the last days is ultimately the same as the decision faced by generations of Christian martyrs in the last two thousand years. Jesus commanded, "And fear not them which kill the body, but are not able to kill the soul: but rather fear him which is able to destroy both soul and body in hell" (Matthew 10:28). Christ's warning to believers about the deception of Satan has never changed: "But whosoever shall deny me before men, him will I also deny before my Father which is in heaven" (Matthew 10:33).

CHAPTER 12

THE ANTICHRIST AND PLANS FOR GLOBAL WAR

*The Coming Global Government Will Be Opposed
by a Devastating Rebellion*

The battle of Armageddon, the coming cataclysmic final world war, will involve the armies of every nation on earth. The Bible declares that at Armageddon, Jesus Christ will destroy the Western armies of the Antichrist and False Prophet together with the two-hundred-million-man army of the kings of the east. Then He will establish His Messianic Kingdom on earth forever.

Much of the catastrophic warfare will focus on the Middle East and Israel. A sign that the final conflict is quickly approaching will be a false seven-year treaty that the Antichrist will sign with the leaders of Israel, promising peace in the Middle East.

> And he shall confirm the covenant with many for one week: and in the midst of the week he shall cause the sacrifice and the oblation to cease, and for the overspreading of abominations he shall make it desolate, even until the consummation, and that determined shall be poured upon the desolate. (Daniel 9:27)

The Lord promised the Holy Land to Abraham and his descendants forever. "Lift up now thine eyes, and look from the place where thou art northward, and southward, and eastward, and westward: For all the land which thou seest, to thee will I give it, and to thy seed forever" (Genesis 13:14–15). For thousands of years Jews have fought and died defending their Promised Land from a long series of pagan invaders. On May 15, 1948, after almost two thousand years of exile, the Jews returned to their land to establish their own nation. This fulfilled numerous prophecies. "And I will make them one nation in the land upon the mountains of Israel" (Ezekiel 37:22).

However, as foretold by Isaiah and Daniel, future leaders of Israel will surrender their national sovereignty to the rising European superpower and its brilliant leader, the Antichrist. He will consolidate his rule throughout the globe using a series of peace treaties followed by military attacks. "By peace [he] shall destroy many" (Daniel 8:25). Similar tactics were used by Adolf Hitler in the years leading up to World War II. John described the coming Antichrist in these words: "And I saw, and behold a white horse: and he that sat on him had a bow; and a crown was given unto him: and he went forth conquering, and to conquer" (Revelation 6:2). The "white horse" and its conquering rider represent the desperate quest for peace and tell how the coming Antichrist will conquer through the willingness of weak national leaders to seek peace at any cost.

After conquering numerous nations through deceptive peace treaties (see Daniel 8:25), the man of sin will unleash his overwhelming military power against the remaining independent nations. His military campaigns will succeed due to his satanic intelligence and power. As Revelation 13:4 states, "They worshipped the beast, saying, Who is like unto the beast? who is able to make war with him?" The extent of his military victories is described in Revelation 13:7: "And it was given unto him to make war with the saints, and to overcome them: and power was given him over all kindreds, and tongues, and nations." The Antichrist will use his evil power to conquer every nation on earth.

SATAN IN THE TEMPLE

Since the creation of humanity, Satan has attempted to replace God in the hearts of men and women. In the beginning "God created man in his own image, in the image of God created he him; male and female created he them" (Genesis 1:27). Since humanity was created in God's image, Satan's greatest triumph would be to deceive humanity to motivate them to worship and follow him as god after rejecting Jesus Christ as the Son of God.

The Antichrist will use his political and military power until the midpoint of the seven-year Tribulation period. During the first three and a half years, he will use his alliance with Mystery Babylon, the false ecumenical New World Religion, to consolidate his power through vast religious propaganda. The world's first truly global faith community will comprise all religious denominations and groups, which will be combined after the Christians have been raptured.

Any religious groups still on earth that wish to survive under the rule of the Antichrist will be forced to join the ecumenical New World Religion. They will be required to acknowledge the supremacy of the neopagan faith over any previous religious traditions and doctrines. Although Mystery Babylon will use Christian symbols to deceive worshipers, the real beliefs and practices will be pagan and satanic in origin. Only those pagan doctrines consistent with the ancient religion of Mystery Babylon will be approved. Any manifestation of genuine faith in God will be ruthlessly suppressed by the religious censors, the secret police of the false church, and the forces of the Antichrist. During this time, however, the ancient Jewish practice of daily animal sacrifices will be allowed to continue at the Temple in Jerusalem, under the terms of a seven-year covenant between the Antichrist and the State of Israel (see Daniel 9:24–27).

After tolerating Temple worship for three and a half years, the Antichrist will "make war with the saints" (Revelation 13:7) during the balance of his evil rule. The book of Daniel warns about this crisis at the midpoint of the seven years when the Antichrist, the "prince that shall come," will stop the daily sacrifice of lambs on the altar in front of the rebuilt Temple (see Daniel 9:26–27).

And from the time that the daily sacrifice shall be taken away, and the abomination that maketh desolate set up, there shall be a thousand two hundred and ninety days. (Daniel 12:11)

Daniel's prophecy indicates that the world dictator will stop the Temple sacrifice three and a half years (1,290 days) before the seven-year Tribulation ends at the battle of Armageddon. In that battle Jesus Christ will utterly defeat the Antichrist, the False Prophet, and the armies of the East and West.

GOD'S WARNING TO TRIBULATION SAINTS

The Bible gives Tribulation saints clues to the identity of the Antichrist, a name that will have a numeric value equal to 666. Jewish and Gentile believers alive during the persecution of the Great Tribulation will have a method to determine the Antichrist's identity and his true spiritual character. John warned Tribulation believers to reject taking the number 666, the Mark of the Beast, so as not to give allegiance to the Antichrist. Without this warning, Tribulation saints could be deceived into worshiping the messianic impostor. Jesus warned, "For there shall arise false Christs, and false prophets, and shall shew great signs and wonders; insomuch that, if it were possible, they shall deceive the very elect" (Matthew 24:24).

The False Prophet will demand that all people accept the Antichrist as their god. Meanwhile, the Antichrist will present himself as the long-awaited messiah by performing "signs and wonders" (Matthew 24:24), supernatural satanic miracles, and satanic deceptions. According to Revelation 13, the "second beast," the False Prophet, will falsely present himself as Elijah the prophet by means of his miraculous satanic power to bring fire down from heaven. As John prophesied, "And he doeth great wonders, so that he maketh fire come down from heaven on the earth in the sight of men" (Revelation 13:13). The only Old Testament prophet to bring fire down from heaven was Elijah.

The False Prophet can perform satanic miracles only when he is in the presence of the Antichrist. Unlike God, who is omnipresent (simultaneously present everywhere at once), Satan, as a fallen angel, can exert his power only in one place at a time. Since Satan will possess the body of the Antichrist, the Antichrist can empower his evil partner, the False Prophet, only when he is very close to him physically.

WARS AND RUMORS OF WARS

On the Mount of Olives, Jesus Christ warned His disciples: "And ye shall hear of wars and rumours of wars: see that ye be not troubled: for all these things must come to pass, but the end is not yet. For nation shall rise against nation, and kingdom against kingdom" (Matthew 24:6–7).

Twenty-five centuries ago, Joel received a vision concerning this final conflict. He prophesied, "Proclaim ye this among the Gentiles; Prepare war, wake up the mighty men, let all the men of war draw near; let them come up: Beat your plowshares into swords, and your pruning hooks into spears: let the weak say, I am strong" (Joel 3:9–10). Throughout history, humanity has endured thirteen years of war for every year of peace. However, since 1945 the number of wars has increased tremendously. As dozens of new nations demanded independence and many old empires disintegrated, more than 350 wars have been fought between World War II and the current time.

The War Atlas, a military study, concluded that the world has not known a single day since World War II without some nation waging war or engaging in a form of armed conflict.[1] Despite thousands of negotiations and peace treaties, the twentieth century was truly the century of war. As a result of the obvious dangers to national security, most nations have joined military alliances to protect themselves. Far more sobering than the increasing frequency of war and terrorist acts is the fact that modern weapons research and enormous military budgets have combined to produce devastating weapons of mass destruction. In the next major war, it is virtually certain that millions of people will be destroyed.

The standing armies of the world contain hundreds of millions of soldiers. The major powers could mobilize and quickly train hundreds of millions of additional troops from National Guard divisions and military reserves in a time of widespread crisis and anticipated war.

The military spending of all nations combined exceeds one and a half trillion dollars in annual expenditures and has been rising in recent years. The United States accounts for nearly 50 percent of the global military spending, according to the research site Global Issues.[2] It is difficult to comprehend the full impact of the fact that humanity invests more than one and a half trillion dollars annually in preparation for war. While many Americans believe that almost 24 percent of the federal budget is spent on foreign aid to help the most disadvantaged, the actual amount spent on foreign aid is less than 2 percent.[3]

According to the report "Reshaping International Order," issued by the Club of Rome, almost 50 percent (some 500,000) of all the scientists in the world focus on advanced weapons research. Almost 40 percent of the world's scientific research funding is devoted to advanced weapons research. Approximately 180 million people were killed in wars and other conflicts during just the twentieth century.[4]

Since 1945, ten nations, including Israel, have built more than seventy thousand nuclear warheads for their growing atomic arsenals. "Vertical proliferation has been under reasonable control after the peak of the Cold War. At that time the United States and Russia combined possessed about 70,000 nuclear weapons; that number has shrunk to about 25,000 nuclear weapons today."[5] If only a small fraction of this enormous investment were redirected toward peaceful purposes, beating "swords into plowshares," we could almost certainly permanently solve the third world's food, water, sanitation, and health problems within a few years.[6]

The enormous armament factories of Russia, China, and the Western nations are producing sophisticated conventional and advanced weaponry at an awesome rate. China is the world's fifth-largest weapons supplier—after Russia, the United States, Britain, and France—selling billions of weapons annually. Chinese-manufactured weapons often are direct copies of either Western or Russian arms but are much cheaper. China is fueling a massive arms race in the

Middle East, with enormous sales of sophisticated tactical missiles and knock-offs of more expensive but still efficient Russian rifles, tanks, and planes. China has in recent years sold more armaments and tanks to poor African nations than all of the Western nations combined.[7]

A poor African nation can buy four Chinese T-59 tanks for the price of one American M1 tank. China and North Korea also are selling intermediate-range missile systems to many Arab regimes. North Korea has sold its own nuclear technology to Iran and Syria.[8] Iran possesses long-range missiles capable of destroying European and Middle Eastern cities and military bases in Israel, Egypt, Saudi Arabia, Turkey, and southern Europe with biological, chemical, and possibly nuclear warheads. Unlike American or European arms suppliers, China and North Korea make no demands whatsoever on how the purchasers will use the weapons. For the first time since the end of the Middle Ages, Europe faces a formidable and determined military threat from Iran and the Muslim Arab world. According to a report in the *Haaretz Daily*, "Iran has received its first batch of North Korean-made surface-to-surface missiles that put European countries within firing range.... The BM-25 missiles have a range of 1,550 miles and are capable of carrying nuclear warheads." The information was attributed to Israel's military intelligence chief.[9]

Despite the 1925 Geneva Protocol against chemical and biological warfare, many nations have stockpiled enormous quantities of biological and chemical doomsday weapons. Countries conduct chemical weapons research based on a clause in the 1925 Geneva Protocol that allows limited research for defensive purposes. However, it is impossible to verify whether research on a chemical or biological weapon in a secret lab is geared for national defense or intended to be used in invading an enemy nation. Russia, China, Syria, Iraq, Egypt, and Iran are developing advanced chemical weapons programs.[10]

The Arab War Against Israel

Many of the leaders in the Muslim nations of Iran, Syria, Yemen, Egypt, Saudi Arabia, and the nations of North Africa are committed to the destruction of

Israel. Not only that, these national leaders want to eliminate all Jews and Christians, as well as moderate Muslims who do not embrace their extremist version of Islam.

From the rebirth of the State of Israel until today, the Israelis have not known peace. Despite years of peace negotiations between the Palestinians, the Arab states, and Israel since 1948, none of the underlying reasons that would trigger a new Arab-Israeli war have been eliminated.

Given the advances in weapons technology and the proliferation of weapons of mass destruction, the coming Middle East war between Iran and its Arab allies against Israel may well include the use of nuclear, chemical, and biological weapons. To put the military crisis in perspective, the twenty-one Arab nations surrounding Israel have accumulated more than three times the number of artillery vehicles and tanks possessed by the combined armies of NATO.[11]

The United States has sold staggering numbers of M1 Abrams tanks, advanced antitank missiles, sophisticated communications systems, and F-22 and F-35 fighter jets to Arab states that remain publicly dedicated to the destruction of the Jewish population of the Israel. The *Independent* declared, "The US has announced military aid packages worth more than $60bn (£30bn) for Israel, Egypt, Saudi Arabia and other key Arab allies in the Gulf. The aim is to boost regional defences against the growing power of Iran and to induce the Saudis in particular to cut back support for Sunni insurgent groups inside Iraq."[12] The Arab nations, with more than two hundred million citizens, face no significant military threat from neighboring states other than the small state of Israel and Iran, with its growing nuclear ambitions.

Israel's population of seven million citizens is less than 0.1 percent of the earth's entire population of over six billion people. Israel, a nation that in area is slightly smaller than New Jersey, is surrounded by twenty-one Arab nations. Together with Iran, the Arab nations have amassed an enormous number of soldiers, exceeding the combined number of soldiers in NATO's military forces by more than a million troops. The only rational reason for the Arab states and Iran to maintain such massive military forces is their shared commitment to annihilate Israel. Jesus Christ prophesied that the Antichrist's armies, represented by the red horseman of the Apocalypse, will ride forth to destroy the population of many nations during the Great Tribulation (see Revelation 6:3–4). Even now we can hear the approaching hoofbeats.

Preparations for a Global War

Many politicians of key nations believe the only way to prevent a devastating global war is for every country to surrender its sovereignty to a world government. Although humanity is desperately seeking peace, the Antichrist will be able to arrange only a very short period of false peace.

John revealed that the first of the Four Horsemen of the Apocalypse would be a rider carrying a bow on a white horse, suggesting military strength and authority. "I saw, and behold a white horse: and he that sat on him had a bow; and a crown was given unto him: and he went forth conquering, and to conquer" (Revelation 6:2). This represents the Antichrist impersonating the Prince of Peace, Jesus Christ, who will ultimately appear riding on a white horse during His triumphant return to earth (see Revelation 19:11). The Antichrist will use humanity's deep natural longing for peace "to conquer" the nations of the world and force them to join his world government.

Muslim states, including Libya, Iran, Syria, and Iraq, have spent untold billions in a desperate attempt to acquire the nuclear warheads that would allow them to destroy Israel and her strongest ally, America. In response, Israel has developed more than three hundred nuclear weapons over the last few decades, including sophisticated neutron bombs capable of destroying targets with nuclear radiation but without creating large explosions.[13]

The world's nations are setting the stage for the final battle of Armageddon, which will drench the world in blood.

THE BATTLE OF ARMAGEDDON

For thousands of years the word *Armageddon* has instilled fear while inspiring the imaginations of millions. While the word itself appears only once in the Bible, hundreds of passages throughout the Scriptures refer to the cataclysmic battle between East and West. John wrote, "And he gathered them together into a place called in the Hebrew tongue Armageddon" (Revelation 16:16). This great final battle will take place in northern Israel and extend southward down the great Valley of Jezreel, below Mount Carmel and the ancient city of Megiddo.

The name *Armageddon* is from the Hebrew word *har* for "mountain" and *Megiddo,* the name of the ancient city built by King Solomon almost three thousand years ago. The city overlooks an enormous plain. This area also is known in the Bible as the valley of Jehoshaphat, meaning "the valley of God's judgment" (see Joel 3:2). According to Revelation 16:16, this ancient battle-ground will be the scene of the most devastating military confrontation in history. While the world will experience intense conflict throughout the final years of the Tribulation period, the final battle will occur in the north of Israel.

The two-hundred-million-man army of the Asian alliance, "the kings of the east," will wage war against the Western armies of the nations loyal to the Antichrist. This battle will be concentrated in a two-hundred-mile-long valley that extends southward from the ancient ruins of Megiddo toward Jerusalem. The carnage will be so terrible that horses will sink into the resulting mire of blood, bodies, and mud until the blood reaches "to the horse bridles" (see Revelation 14:19–20).

By that time it is not likely that Russia will still be a superpower. Most of its armies will have been destroyed previously during the battle of Gog and Magog. That battle will most likely take place before the seven-year Tribulation period, when Russia and its Eastern European allies together with the Islamic nations invade Israel. According to Ezekiel, the nations that join in this Arab confederacy will be destroyed. God will attack them supernaturally using earthquakes, plagues, hailstones, and fire from heaven—as well as confusing the units of their armies so that they end up killing one another (see Ezekiel 38–39).

The Armies of Armageddon

In the last years of the Tribulation period, the only remaining major political-military superpower will be a combination of the vast populations and industrial-military capabilities of China, Southeast Asia, and India, aided by the technological and economic leadership of a remilitarized Japan. In 2001 the leaders of China, Kazakhstan, Kyrgyzstan, Russia, Tajikistan, and Uzbekistan joined the Shanghai Cooperation Organisation, which was formed by a group of Asian nations committed to mutual economic and military defense. Iran has joined this alliance, which helps explain the support of Russia and China for Iran's plans to develop a nuclear weapons program.

The Antichrist will visit his headquarters in Jerusalem at some point in the final years of his seven-year rule as world dictator. At that point an alliance of Muslim, African, and Arab nations will be formed, led by a "king of the south" (perhaps Egypt). Another group of rebel nations, led by a "king of the north" (probably Syria), will attack the Antichrist's armies in Israel. After the forces of the Antichrist repel both of these attacks, the Antichrist's armies will conquer Egypt, Libya, and Ethiopia (see Daniel 11:40–43).

Meanwhile, the major nations of Asia will grow weary of being subjugated and will attack the Antichrist's armies in Israel. The powerful nations of the Far East (perhaps including China, India, and Japan; see Daniel 11:44–45) and the north (perhaps the remaining parts of Siberia) will mobilize their vast armies for this final decisive battle.

John prophesied, "And the sixth angel poured out his vial upon the great river Euphrates; and the water thereof was dried up, that the way of the kings of the east might be prepared" (Revelation 16:12). To make it possible for the two-hundred-million-man invading army (see Revelation 9:16) to cross from Asia into the Middle East, the Euphrates River will dry up.

During the battle of Armageddon, Jesus Christ will save Israel from total destruction. Christ will destroy the Western armies of the Antichrist and the armies of the kings of the east. John described Christ's final victory:

> And I saw heaven opened, and behold a white horse; and he that sat
> upon him was called Faithful and True, and in righteousness he doth
> judge and make war. His eyes were as a flame of fire, and on his head
> were many crowns; and he had a name written, that no man knew, but

he himself. And he was clothed with a vesture dipped in blood: and his name is called The Word of God. And the armies which were in heaven followed him upon white horses, clothed in fine linen, white and clean. And out of his mouth goeth a sharp sword, that with it he should smite the nations: and he shall rule them with a rod of iron: and he treadeth the winepress of the fierceness and wrath of Almighty God. And he hath on his vesture and on his thigh a name written, KING OF KINGS, AND LORD OF LORDS. (Revelation 19:11–16)

The Unprecedented Asian Army

When John prophesied that the kings of the east would marshal an army of two hundred million men (see Revelation 9:16), the entire population of the Roman Empire was approximately one hundred million men, women, and children. Over the centuries it has been difficult for many Bible commentators to take the two-hundred-million number literally. Prior to World War II, only twelve battles in history were fought with more than fifty thousand soldiers on both sides. But in the late twentieth century, The War Atlas reported that a worldwide military census could account for armies that, combined, could potentially call up five hundred million soldiers.[14]

For thousands of years the male-female balance within national populations remained virtually static, with the number of men roughly equaling the number of women. But in the late twentieth and early twenty-first centuries, political decrees, prenatal exams, the selective abortion of females, and economic selfishness produced an extreme gender imbalance among the 1.3 billion people in China. Chinese officials I spoke with in 1986 admitted that the one-child-per-family policy was essential to avoid a future famine. However, because female fetuses often are aborted by couples who prefer their one child to be a son, China faces an extreme imbalance in population between boys and girls. In excess of one hundred million young men have no hope of finding wives or enjoying a conventional home life.

At the same time China has been fighting a wave of kidnappings and abductions of women and girls. Tens of thousands of women are bought and sold in China each year. From 1991 through 1996, Chinese police freed eighty-eight thousand kidnapped women and female children. "Local authorities do not assist the victims because they have sympathy for men who cannot find wives."[15] By 2009, the gender-based population imbalance favored males by more than one hundred million.[16] A similar phenomenon is being reported in India and other Asian countries. This means that John's prophecy of a two-hundred-million-man army from the "kings of the east" is not only literally possible, it is virtually certain.

At the conclusion of this final battle, Jesus will return from heaven with His heavenly army—hundreds of millions of resurrected saints (see Jude 14–15), plus legions of angels. Christ will destroy the Antichrist, the False Prophet, and their Western armies, as well as the military forces of the kings of the east. The Lord will rescue all those who repent of their sinful rebellion and call upon His name for divine protection (see Zechariah 12:1–9). And at the end of the battle, Christ will set up His Kingdom on earth forever.

PART 4

SECRET PLANS TO CONTROL THE WORLD'S ECONOMY

CHAPTER 13

EVIDENCE OF THE GLOBALIST ECONOMIC STRATEGY

International Economic Strategies Against America

As a consequence of international trade, the economies of individual countries long ago became dependent on doing business beyond their own borders. As we witnessed in 2008 and 2009, a global economic collapse transformed the economic expectations of world leaders. The pervasiveness of global commerce and international investment has transformed the balance of power in the world.

The Industrial Revolution established the economic, political, and military supremacy of the Western nations. The ability of European nations and the United States to generate power from water, steam, and petroleum drove the industrialization that gave rise to the steel industry, the automobile industry, shipbuilding, air transportation, and other industries that quickly dominated markets worldwide. In more recent years, the manufacturing economy gave way to the digital economy, with information becoming a leading commodity. Technology to send, store, retrieve, search for, and disseminate information has advanced much more rapidly than did the leading products of the Industrial Revolution. And once again, the West (with strong competition from Japan) led the way.

The awesome industrial machine based in the Western nations created national wealth by producing massive quantities of goods, used both in peacetime economies and military industries. After World War II, as the United States returned to a peacetime economy, the focus shifted to massive investments in research and development, rapid adoption of computerized machinery, fiberoptic communications networks, and advanced military equipment. During that time, Asian nations—including Japan, Taiwan, South Korea, and now India and mainland China—embarked on a very effective catch-up campaign with the West. In many cases, other countries accelerated their technological progress by using industrial espionage to steal research, formulas, computer codes, and industrial secrets.

In the digital age, a nation's level of industrialization means far less than does its ability to produce, control, and protect technological information. Knowledge and the ability to leverage information to one's own advantage now determine who controls the world's economy and, by extension, who rules the globe. George A. Keyworth, the science advisor to President Ronald Reagan, wrote, "We're moving increasingly toward a business environment in which information itself is the product, and in which the strategies by which businesses use information become critical elements of their success or failure."[1]

ECONOMIC WARFARE

The General Agreement on Tariffs and Trade (GATT), the North American Free Trade Agreement (NAFTA), and the World Trade Organization (WTO) are leading the nations of the world toward a one-world government. The international trade agreements shifted control over the economic future of the United States and Canada to foreign officials and organizations that do not share our capitalist values or our love of free enterprise. Multinational corporations worked behind the scenes, spending vast sums of money and employing thousands of lobbyists, to make sure Congress and the White House adopted trade agreements that serve the corporations' globalist agendas.

For example, the basic philosophy behind GATT and the WTO is to reduce the tariffs imposed by nations trying to protect their industries against inexpensive foreign imports. In the case of textiles, the reduction of tariffs could destroy an entire U.S. industry. The WTO advanced a plan that allowed foreign manufacturers in countries such as China, that pay workers only 5 percent of the average wages of American workers, to sell cheap textiles in American stores, thereby destroying the jobs of a million American textile workers.

THE WORLD BANK AND THE INTERNATIONAL MONETARY FUND

The World Bank Group, which is controlled by the United Nations, is composed of several key entities. One is the International Bank for Reconstruction and Development (IBRD), which is the main lending department of the World Bank. Another is the International Development Association (IDA), the World Bank affiliate that lends money to the world's poorest nations. The operations of the World Bank provide a clear picture of the globalist strategy to consolidate power through the use and control of international finance. As it pertains to finance, the World Bank and the International Monetary Fund (IMF) are forcing countries to follow the monetary rules of the New World Order.

The World Bank and the IMF use the "carrot" of promised new loans and the "stick" of delayed approval of debt restructuring for a nation's past loans. In this way, they force the leaders of third world nations to obey the dictates of the globalist elite. In practice, it often looks like this: a country is burdened with a crushing interest rate and disadvantageous terms of repayment. The country now owes such a massive debt that it has no hope of ever repaying the loans. At that point, the IMF might offer more favorable terms of repayment in exchange for that country's approval of an IMF-favored trade agreement. In the Trilateral Commission's Task Force Report #39, globalist writers declared their intentions: "With due deference to local circumstances and sensibilities, the Trilateral countries should be frank in advocating the need for reform and modernization of Latin American economies. Such efforts are necessary both to achieve recovery and secure international support—particularly from the Trilateral private sector."[2]

THE THREAT OF NAFTA

Since the adoption of NAFTA, North American multinational corporations have moved thousands of factories to Mexico and South America, outsourcing millions of jobs in the process. Relocating factories is worth the expense because operating costs are so much lower outside the United States. In Mexico, for example, the minimum wage is less than eighty cents per hour with few pension benefits, negligible healthcare coverage, and virtually nonexistent safety and environmental regulations. For years, the Big Three automakers have paid wages that are more than 50 percent higher than comparable assembly-line wages paid by foreign auto manufacturers. The remarkably low wages paid in Mexico, South America, and Asia put companies that keep their operations in the United States or Canada at a tremendous competitive disadvantage.

With NAFTA in place, the incentive is even greater to move manufacturing outside the country. Guess where the board of the multinational company will choose to build its next plant, especially when the company can avoid most corporate taxes by locating in a foreign jurisdiction? After manufacturing goods overseas, the multinationals ship the low-cost products back to the United States for sale to American consumers at prices no U.S. manufacturing corporation can match. Welcome to the world of free trade.

Former U.S. Secretary of State Henry Kissinger, a leading member of the Trilateral Commission, was one of the architects of the New World Order. As an expert in diplomacy, Kissinger is an authority on the true intent of international treaties. Listen to his evaluation of the real meaning of NAFTA: "What the Congress will soon have before it is not a conventional trade agreement, but the hopeful architecture of a new international system. A regional Western Hemisphere Organization dedicated to democracy and free trade would be a first step towards the New World Order that is so frequently cited but so rarely implemented."[3]

THE DANGER POSED BY THE WTO

The globalist elite want to reduce and eventually eliminate America's independence and national sovereignty. And step by step, the U.S. economy is being placed under the control of international interests. International trade agreements already have transferred significant control of the American economy away from Congress and into the hands of the 153-member-nation WTO. The WTO was created at the conclusion of the Uruguay Round of negotiations to replace GATT.

Under the previous GATT system, the United States could impose trade sanctions and restrictions as part of a diplomatic campaign against a nation that was violating its citizens' human rights. While this was technically against the rules of international trade, GATT had no legal capability to penalize America. However, under current rules of international trade, America must follow the rules imposed by the WTO. If the United States violates these rules by unilaterally imposing trade sanctions, the WTO will impose trade sanctions on American exports. These restrictions on U.S. economic policy can severely limit the options of an American president to influence another country's actions. This represents one more significant surrender of national sovereignty in preparation for the coming one-world government.

A careful study of history reveals that whoever controls a nation's currency and economy controls that nation. Power-hungry bureaucrats at the United Nations and their globalist friends in the European Union and the WTO are delighted with the prospect of gaining control over the U.S. economy.

Without question NAFTA and the WTO pose a threat to American sovereignty. But to an even greater extent, the WTO puts the U.S. economy at risk. The ostensible purpose of the WTO is to liberalize trade relations among nations by lowering tariffs and opening markets. Based in Geneva, Switzerland, the WTO replaced GATT with a mandate to strictly enforce international trade rules. But the real purpose is to put some teeth into the rules of the international trade organization.

In the past a country that didn't like a GATT ruling could ignore it and impose tariffs or sanctions as it saw fit to protect its national interests. But with the WTO, such an option has disappeared. An article in the *New American* explained why: "The truth is that the WTO bureaucracy would have sufficient power to pressure nations to change their domestic laws. WTO was designed to eliminate a nation's option to ignore GATT dispute panel rulings, as the United States had done in an August 1991 case."[4]

This attack on the federal government's independent control of America's economy is contained in a treaty that is so complicated that the document includes twenty-two thousand pages of text! If the true intent of the WTO was simply to reduce tariffs, this could be expressed in one page of text. Obviously, hidden in the tens of thousands of pages of legal language are thousands of special exceptions and lucrative deals for multinational companies whose lobbyists worked for years to bring this agreement to fruition. Any nation that is found to be in violation of the decisions of the WTO dispute panel will find itself hauled before the world body and forced to change its laws or pay massive fines or face worldwide trade sanctions. In all of history there has never been such an attack against the sovereignty and independence of the nation-state.

Other international organizations, such as the UN Security Council, allow America and the other superpowers to protect their national interests through a veto over actions they perceive as being against their national interest. However, in the WTO, every state in the world, including small nations such as Mongolia and Monaco, has the same voting power as the United States. In a trade dispute, America has no veto power and only one vote among the 153 nations in the WTO.

Phyllis Schlafly, president of the conservative political group Eagle Forum, commented on the real motivation of the globalists who pushed for the WTO. She wrote, "The WTO is designed to function as the global trade pillar of a triumvirate that will plan and control the world's economy.... The World Bank and the IMF got off the ground rapidly (largely financed, of course, by the United States), but the planned global trade arm, then called the International Trade Organization (ITO), was blocked by U.S. senators who concluded that it would diminish U.S. sovereignty and interfere with U.S. domestic laws."[5]

NAFTA ANTICIPATES THE NEW WORLD ORDER

As an example of the covert economic agenda of the New World Order, consider NAFTA, the trade agreement between the United States, Canada, and Mexico. President George H. W. Bush spoke to a group of Latin American diplomats and American bankers in the White House, promising, "I want to assure all of you here today, as I've assured many democratic leaders in Central and South America and the Caribbean and Mexico, the United States will not lose sight of the tremendous challenges and opportunities right here in our own hemisphere."[6]

In order to achieve global domination, it is essential that the leaders of the superpowers first achieve regional dominance. The New World Order will begin by dominating the various regions of the globe, starting with the Western Hemisphere. The world is being divided into three spheres of influence, each headed by one of the three major global economic players. Those players are, first, the United States as the world's largest economy with a gross national product (GNP) of $13.8 trillion in 2007 (dominating North, Central and South America). Second, the twenty-seven nations of the European Union with a GNP of $16.9 trillion (dominating Europe, the Middle East, and Africa). And third, Japan with a GNP of $4.3 trillion (the second largest economy in the world) will dominate Asia. While China's economy is growing rapidly, China's GNP in 2007 was still less than one-quarter the size of the U.S. economy.

NAFTA has produced massive economic changes. However, a much more extensive free trade zone arrangement is in the works that will encompass the whole of the Western Hemisphere, from the southern tip of South America to the North Pole. Huge multinational companies will be able to produce goods in every country without high taxes, duties, or customs. Additionally, they will not have to pay for employee healthcare coverage, pensions, or the higher wages required to attract skilled North American workers. Many more plants and jobs will inevitably move south of the Rio Grande faster than they do at present.

Who is pushing for these agreements when it is so obvious that average American and Canadian workers are being harmed? Naturally, it is the huge financial and multinational corporations, and the politicians they financially support, pushing us closer and closer to the New World Order.

If nations refuse to join the proposed global government, they will be left out in the cold. And if they do join, they will lose control of their independent economic and, ultimately, political destiny. The price that countries must pay for the privilege to sit at the table of the new global government is fourfold:

- Accept a global free-market economy.
- Pay off all international bank debts as demanded by the IMF and the World Bank.
- Privatize all nationalized industries.
- Remove all barriers to Western investment and trade.

That represents a very high price indeed.

Opposition to international trade agreements is growing in Canada and the United States among concerned citizens, union workers, and environmentalists. They fear, correctly, that our craven politicians and business leaders are selling out our corporations and workers, together with our national interests, in secret backroom agreements. International trade agreements harm individuals and national economies but greatly benefit the interests of the globalist elite.

PREPARING FOR THE LAST DAYS

The evidence presented in *Shadow Government* confirms the accuracy of biblical prophecy. Thousands of years ago the prophets foretold that in the last days the world's nations would join together in a global government. Further, God's prophets predicted that the Roman Empire would be revived in a unique superstate composed of ten major nations. Finally, the Bible foretold that in the last days a world dictator would rise, one who would be able to control the allegiance of everyone on earth, "small and great, rich and poor, free and bond" (Revelation 13:16).

For the first time in history, it is possible for the ancient prophecies to be fulfilled. Every action of every person is now being monitored as new surveillance technologies allow governments to watch, record, and use information about the activities and economic transactions of each citizen. Because of our loss of privacy, humanity stands at a crossroads.

The decisions made by individuals and government leaders will determine whether surveillance technology will be used to improve the lot of humanity or whether it will be turned against us and used to enslave us. The tools already exist to equip the coming global government with everything it needs to create the totalitarian surveillance nightmare described in the books of Daniel and Revelation.

The nightmare will end only when the Lord Jesus Christ returns from heaven to defeat the forces of the Antichrist. Those who love their freedom and privacy need to be aware of the growing dangers, and they need to alert their representatives in government to the threats posed by these technologies. We also need to oppose all policies that weaken and destroy our freedom. Jesus warned His disciples, "When ye shall see all these things, know that it is near, even at the doors. Verily I say unto you, This generation shall not pass, till all these things be fulfilled" (Matthew 24:33–34).

The first major prophetic warning in the Bible was given to Noah before the Flood that destroyed virtually all life on the planet. For 120 years Noah, called the "preacher of righteousness" (2 Peter 2:5; see also Genesis 6), warned his evil generation of God's coming judgment. However, despite the fact that Noah spent more than a century building a huge ark, demonstrating his faith in God's prophecy of the coming global flood, the entire population rejected God's warning. Even when Noah, his family, and the chosen animals entered the ark, Noah's neighbors still refused to believe. Picture those who failed to heed the warning. For more than a hundred years, they had watched a man of faith build an unprecedented ark. But in spite of Noah's obedience to God and his family's commitment, the onlookers still refused to accept his prophetic warnings. When the rain began to fall and the waters began to rise, those who had rejected Noah's warning realized they had been wrong. However, the door of the ark was shut. Noah's generation had knowingly rejected God's message, presented to them by Noah's century of ark building as well as his warnings. Tragically, that generation of untold millions of unrepentant sinners died in the Flood.

The message of prophecy is vital to the Church in these last days for four basic reasons.

The first is that the accuracy of the fulfillment of the prophetic message proves the inspiration of the Scriptures and validates the message of Jesus Christ as the inspired Word of God.

Second, the prophecies call on Christians to live in holiness in an immoral world. The New Testament tells us that the hope of the Second Coming of Christ demands that Christians live in holiness while awaiting His return. "And every man that hath this hope in him purifieth himself, even as he is pure" (1 John 3:3).

The third reason is this: prophecy is vital in that it encourages Christians to witness with urgency to their friends, neighbors, and family while they still have time to accept Jesus as their Lord and Savior. The apostle John warns us with Jesus' words that we have only a limited time to share our faith with others. Jesus said, "I must work the works of him that sent me, while it is day: the night cometh, when no man can work" (John 9:4). Jesus urgently witnessed to His generation because He knew they were approaching the prophesied destruction of Jerusalem and Israel in A.D. 70. Likewise, our generation is quickly approaching the time of the Second Coming of Christ. Our opportunity to witness to those around us is limited. In light of the soon coming of our Lord, we need to witness with urgency to our generation.

The fourth reason is that prophecy is the most effective way available to us to witness to friends and family who have not yet found faith in Jesus. There is an inborn curiosity in every human heart about the future and how it will unfold. Even those who have never expressed interest in the Christian faith often are fascinated by the fulfillment of prophecy in our generation. And fulfilled prophecy always points to the truthfulness of the Word of God.

SCIENCE AND GOD'S TRUTH

Sir Isaac Newton, one of history's greatest scientists, commented on the tremendous importance of biblical prophecy in his book *Observations upon the Prophecies of Daniel, and the Apocalypse of St. John*:

> The authority of the Prophets is divine, and comprehends the sum of religion.... Their writings contain the covenant between God and his people, with instructions for keeping this covenant; instances of God's judgments upon them that break it: and predictions of things to come....
>
> 'Tis therefore a part of this Prophecy [the book of Revelation], that it should not be understood before the last age of this world; and therefore it makes for the credit of the Prophecy, that it is not yet understood. But if the last age, the age of opening these things, be now approaching,

as by the great successes of late Interpreters it seems to be, we have more encouragement than ever to look into these things....

He gave this and the Prophecies of the Old Testament, not to gratify men's curiosities by enabling them to foreknow things, but so that after that they were fulfilled they might be interpreted by the event, and his own providence, not the interpreters, be then manifested thereby to the world. For the event of things predicted many ages before, will then be a convincing argument that the world is governed by providence.... The event will prove the *Apocalypse;* and this Prophecy, thus proved and understood, will open the old Prophets, and all together will make known the true religion, and establish it.... There is already so much of the Prophecy fulfilled, that as many will take pains in this study, may see sufficient instances of God's providence: but then the signal revolutions predicted by all the holy Prophets, will at once both turn mens [sic] eyes upon considering the predictions, and plainly interpret them.[1]

In 1 Chronicles 12:32 we read a description of an Israelite tribe, "the children of Issachar," who were known as "men that had understanding of the times, to know what Israel ought to do." The tribe of Issachar was noted for their interest in prophecy. They understood by spiritual means the nature of their times and consequently they would "know what Israel ought to do." Our understanding of the prophecies about our generation and the rise of the Antichrist's kingdom should motivate us to become a beacon of light in a dark time. Look around you and you will see people who are searching for any reason to hope. Our hope is in the soon return of Jesus Christ.

THE DECISION IS UP TO YOU

In the preceding chapters, attention has been focused on the remarkable technology of surveillance and on the economic, political, and military developments that are rushing us toward the final world government described in the Word of God. These same incredibly accurate Scriptures prophesied that every one of us will soon face our personal appointment with God. The writer of the book of Hebrews wrote about our personal destiny: "It is appointed unto men once to die, but after this the judgment" (Hebrews 9:27).

The apostle Paul said that God "now commandeth all men every where to repent: Because he hath appointed a day, in the which he will judge the world in righteousness by that man whom he hath ordained; whereof he hath given assurance unto all men, in that he hath raised him from the dead" (Acts 17:30–31).

Every one of us will someday soon come face to face with Jesus Christ to give an account of the decision we have made regarding our relationship with Him. Every one of us has sinned by rebelling against God throughout our lives. The apostle Paul wrote, "For all have sinned, and come short of the glory of God" (Romans 3:23). The consequences of our personal choice to reject God, His grace, and His commandments is that we, as sinners, have become unfit to enter heaven. God's Word declares, "For the wages of sin is death; but the gift of God is eternal life through Jesus Christ our Lord" (Romans 6:23). The Scriptures declare that our sinful rebellion has alienated every one of us from the holiness of God. Our continued rebellion and rejection of Christ will prevent us from ever entering heaven unless our sins are forgiven by God.

The sacrificial death of Jesus on the Cross is the key to bringing us to a place of peace with God. The death of our old sinful nature, as we identify with Christ's death on the Cross, is the key to finding true peace with God. Jesus asked His disciples this vital question, "Whom say ye that I am? And Simon Peter answered and said, Thou art the Christ, the Son of the living God" (Matthew 16:15–16). Every one of us must answer that question for ourselves. Your answer will determine your eternal destiny. If we refuse to answer, we have already rejected Christ's claims to be our Savior.

According to God's Word, the choices we make in this life will have eternal consequences in the next. The apostle Paul wrote, "For it is written, As I live, saith the Lord, every knee shall bow to me, and every tongue shall confess to God. So then every one of us shall give account of himself to God" (Romans 14:11–12). Appearing in front of the throne of God in heaven, every single human will bow his or her knee to Jesus Christ and acknowledge Him as

Almighty God. The question to you is this: Will you choose to repent of your sins now and spiritually bow your knee willingly to your Savior and Lord? Or will you reject His offer of salvation today and finally be forced by His majesty to bow your knee as you face your final Judge, just before you are sent to an eternity in hell?

When we finally meet Christ on Judgment Day, everyone will know whether we accepted or rejected His precious gift of salvation. When Jesus was crucified, He paid the complete price of our sins. His final statement before His death was, "It is finished" (John 19:30). As the sinless Lamb of God, Jesus allowed Himself to be offered as a perfect Sacrifice to pay the price of our sins and to reconcile each of us to God. However, in a manner similar to a pardon offered to a prisoner awaiting execution, each of us must repent of our sins and personally accept Christ's pardon. That is the only way that His salvation will become effective in our lives. Paul the apostle declared, "We shall all stand before the judgment seat of Christ" (Romans 14:10). The basis of God's judgment following our physical death will be our personal relationship with Jesus Christ, not whether we were better or worse than most other people.

God demands perfect holiness and righteousness. However, it is obvious that no person can meet this requirement. Since God could never ignore the fact that we have sinned against Him, it was necessary that Someone who was perfect and sinless should pay the penalty of physical and spiritual death as a substitute for us. The only person who could qualify was Jesus Christ, the Holy Son of God.

One of the righteous religious leaders of Israel, Nicodemus, came to Jesus and asked how he could be certain of his future salvation. Jesus answered, "Verily, verily, I say unto thee, Except a man be born again, he cannot see the kingdom of God" (John 3:3). It isn't simply a matter of intellectually accepting the facts about Christ and salvation.

To be "born again" you must sincerely repent of your sinful life, asking Christ to forgive you, and then you must wholeheartedly trust in Him for the rest of your life. Jesus explained to Nicodemus, "For God so loved the world, that he gave his only begotten Son, that whosoever believeth in him should not perish, but have everlasting life" (John 3:16). The decision to believe in Christ will transform your life forever. God will give you new purpose and meaning. The Lord promises believers eternal life in heaven: "This is the will of him that sent me, that every one which seeth the Son, and believeth on him, may have everlasting life: and I will raise him up at the last day" (John 6:40). The moment you commit your life to Christ, you receive eternal life. Though your body will die, you will live forever with Christ in heaven.

Jesus said, "He that believeth on him [the Son] is not condemned: but he that believeth not is condemned already, because he hath not believed in the name of the only begotten Son of God" (John 3:18). Jesus is the *only* way to God. He said, "I am the way, the truth, and the life: no man cometh unto the Father, but by me" (John 14:6). God declares in these inspired words that there is no other road to salvation. You must accept the "way," the "truth," and the "life" of Jesus Christ.

Every one of us, by accepting His pardon, can stand before the judgment seat of God clothed in Christ's righteousness: "For he [God] hath made him [Jesus] to be sin for us, who knew no sin; that we might be made the righteousness of God in Him" (2 Corinthians 5:21). This fact of Christ's atonement is perhaps the greatest mystery in creation. Jesus is the only One in history who, by His sinless life, was qualified to enter heaven. Yet He loved each one of us so much that He chose to die on the Cross to purchase our salvation. In a marvelous act of God's mercy, the righteousness of Jesus is credited to our spiritual account with God.

It will cost you a great deal to live as a committed Christian. People will challenge your faith. The Lord Jesus Christ asks His disciples to follow Him. Your decision and commitment to Jesus will change your life forever. However, your commitment to Christ also will release His supernatural grace and power to transform your life into one of joy and peace. While the decision to follow Christ will cost you much, it will cost you far more if you do not accept Him as your Savior. Jesus challenges us with these words: "For what shall it profit a man, if he shall gain the whole world, and lose his own soul?" (Mark 8:36).

All people who have accepted Christ are called to be witnesses of Christ's message to the world. To be a faithful witness to Christ demands an active, not a passive, involvement in the lives of your Christian brothers and sisters and the lives of unbelievers. It requires a willingness to pay the price of a personal commitment to your coming Messiah. The imminent Second Coming of Christ should motivate all of us to witness to the unsaved around us. If you are a Christian, I challenge you to share the evidence in this book to witness to your friends and family.

As the prophetic clock ticks on toward the final midnight hour, the invitation of Christ is still open: "Behold, I stand at the door, and knock: if any man hear my voice, and open the door, I will come in to him, and will sup with him, and he with me" (Revelation 3:20).

Many of the readers of this book have already chosen to follow the Lord; I encourage you to obey His Great Commission. In Matthew 28:19–20, Jesus commanded, "Go ye therefore, and teach all nations, baptizing them in the name of the Father, and of the Son, and of the Holy Ghost: Teaching them to observe all things whatsoever I have commanded you: and, lo, I am with you alway, even unto the end of the world."

I wrote this book and my previous books to introduce nonbelievers to faith in Christ and to encourage Christians in their faith. In addition, my goal is to provide believers with books they can give to their friends and neighbors who do not yet have a personal faith in Christ.

The incredible events of the last decade are causing many to ask what lies ahead. There is a growing fascination in North America with Bible prophecies regarding the last days. This tremendous interest in prophecy presents us with a great opportunity to witness to those around us who do not yet know Christ as their personal Savior.

Notes

Introduction

1. Pierre Teilhard de Chardin, quoted in Louis Pauwels and Jacques Bergier, *Morning of the Magicians* (New York: Stein and Day, 1964), 55.

2. See John Buchan, *The Power-House* (London: William Blackwood and Sons, 1916).

3. Isaac Newton, *Observations upon the Prophecies of Daniel, and the Apocalypse of St. John* (London: J. Darby and T. Brown, 1733), 12.

Chapter 1

1. Joseph Farah, "Big Brother Spy Plan Sparks Revolt: Government Wants Every Telephone Registered," WorldNetDaily, October 27, 2008, www.worldnetdaily.com/index.php?fa=PAGE.view&pageId=78858 (accessed March 25, 2009).

2. Marina Hyde, "This Surveillance Onslaught Is Draconian and Creepy," *Guardian* (London), June 28, 2008, www.guardian.co.uk/commentisfree/2008/jun/28/civil liberties.privacy (accessed April 29, 2009).

3. Scott McNealy, quoted in Brock N. Meeks, "Is Privacy Possible in the Digital Age?" MSNBC, December 7, 2000, www.msnbc.msn.com/id/3078854 (accessed March 28, 2009).

4. This example was cited in "Panel: Privacy Doesn't Exist Anymore," *Direct Marketing News,* July 5, 1999, 10.

5. The International Labor Organization in Geneva has strongly criticized computer surveillance of employees. "Workers in industrialized countries are gradually losing privacy in the workplace as technological advances allow employers to monitor nearly every facet of time on the job," said Prathiba Mahanamahewa in his paper "Computer Monitoring in the 21st Century Workplace," University of Colombo, Sri Lanka, 2008, http://icsa.cs.up.ac.za/issa/2008/Proceedings/Full/15.pdf (accessed April 29, 2009).

6. "Stop Snooping," www.bigbrother.org/?main=articles&ID=6 (accessed March 29, 2009).

7. "Canada Scraps Citizen Database," *Wired*, May 30, 2000, www.wired.com/politics/law/news/2000/05/36649 (accessed March 29, 2009).

8. Catherine Yang, Kerry Capell, and Otis Port, "The State of Surveillance," *Business Week*, August 8, 2005, www.businessweek.com/print/magazine/content/05_32/b3946001_mz001.htm?chan=gl (accessed March 29, 2009).

9. In the meantime, you should take practical steps to protect against identity theft and other forms of fraud. To avoid identity theft, at least every three months you should check your personal credit records with the three major credit rating agencies to see if an unfamiliar company has requested credit information on you. If so, consider this a red flag that a thief is probably attempting to apply for credit using your identity. Always check your bank and investment account statements for any suspicious transactions. Never leave your wallet or purse unattended, even in a "safe" place such as at church, at a party, or when visiting in someone's home. When shopping or dining out, watch carefully when a clerk or waiter swipes your credit card. Make sure they are not making a secondary swipe of your credit card for fraudulent use of your credit. And always examine the credit card returned to you to verify that it is your card and not someone else's.

10. Summarized from the European Union Web site's "Directive 95/46/EC of the European Parliament and of the Council of 24 October 1995 on the protection of individuals with regard to the processing of personal data and on the free movement of such data," www.cdt.org/privacy/eudirective/EU_Directive_.html (accessed April 22, 2009).

11. Despite widespread privacy concerns, Donna Farmer, president and CEO of the Smart Card Forum, raises an interesting counterargument. In an article on privacy concerns and smart cards, Farmer suggested that smart cards could assist in the prevention of invasive privacy attacks. "Think of how much information is in the clear in my wallet," she wrote. "On a Smart Card that data would be encrypted. It would be hundreds of times more secure." At the same time, Farmer admitted, "As we move into a digital age, people have to be much more aware of their own personal security." Donna Farmer, "Big Brother Casts a Shadow over Smart Cards," *Card Technology*, March 1999, 1.

12. Stephanie Miles and Stephen Shankland, "PIII Debuts Amid Controversy," CNET News, February 26, 1999, http://news.cnet.com/2100-1040-222256.html (accessed April 29, 2009).

13. Dave Mathews, "Microsoft Attaches an ID to All Office Documents!" Davemathews .com, March 8, 1999, www.davemathews.com/MicrosoftGUID.html (accessed April 29, 2009).

Chapter 2

1. See Scott Shane and Tom Bowman, "No Such Agency, Part 4: Rigging the Game," *Baltimore Sun,* December 4, 1995.

2. J. Orlin Grabbe, "NSA, Crypto AG, and the Iraq-Iran Conflict," November 2, 1997, www.hermetic.ch/crypto/kalliste/speccoll.htm (accessed March 24, 2009).

3. Wayne Madsen, "Crypto AG: The NSA's Trojan Whore?" *Covert Action Quarterly,* http://mediafilter.org/caq/cryptogate (accessed March 24, 2009).

4. Madsen, "Crypto AG."

5. Grabbe, "NSA, Crypto AG, and the Iran-Iraq Conflict."

6. Grabbe, "NSA, Crypto AG, and the Iraq-Iran Conflict."

7. See Madsen, "Crypto AG."

8. Javier Bernal, "Big Brother Is On-Line: Public and Private Security in the Internet," *Cybersociology Magazine* 6, August 6, 1999, www.cybersociology.com/files/6_publicand privatesecurity.html (accessed June 2, 2009).

9. Lucas Mearian, "Internet Archive to Unveil Massive Wayback Machine Data Center," Computerworld, March 19, 2009, www.computerworld.com/action/article.do ?command=viewArticleBasic&taxonomyName=hardware&articleId=9130081& taxonomyId=12&intsrc=kc_top (accessed March 22, 2009).

10. Bruce Schneier, "Crypto-Gram Newsletter," October 15, 1998, www.schneier .com/crypto-gram-9810.html (accessed March 24, 2009). Schneier's sobering warning has been echoed by David Sobel, general counsel to the Electronic Privacy Information Center in Washington DC. In the late 1990s, Sobel warned, "If you define privacy as the right of individuals to control information about themselves—as we do—then mega-archiving systems clearly raise significant privacy issues. These systems convert every passing thought and contemporaneous musing into a permanent, retrievable

record—without, in many cases, the knowledge or consent of the creator." David Sobel, quoted in Joseph D. Lasica, "Your Past Is Your Future, Web-Wise," *Washington Post,* October 11, 1998.

11. After the European Commission advisory body for data protection, called Article 29, suggested that Google's data retention practices might be in violation of European privacy laws, Google announced that it would begin retaining personally identifiable search-engine data for "only one and a half years." See "Google Cuts Data Retention Times," BBC News, June 12, 2007, http://news.bbc.co.uk/2/hi/technology/6745191 .stm (accessed March 30, 2009).

12. Jeffrey Chester, "Google: Search and Data Seizure," *Nation,* September 28, 2007, www.thenation.com/doc/20071015/chester (accessed March 30, 2009).

13. Federal Bureau of Investigation, Reading Room Index, http://foia.fbi.gov/foiaindex/ foiaindex.htm (accessed March 29, 2009).

Chapter 3

1. "Electronic Product Code (EPC): An Overview," EPCglobal, www.epcglobalinc .org/public/ppsc_factsheets/epc_overview (accessed March 30, 2009).

2. Lori Valigra, "Smart Tags: Shopping Will Never Be the Same," *Christian Science Monitor,* March 29, 2001, www.csmonitor.com/2001/0329/p13s1.html (accessed March 24, 2009).

3. "The Electronic Product Code: A Technology Revolution in the Making," *eRetail Report,* April 2001, www.bizbrick.com/eretailnews/issues/ern2001-4.pdf (accessed March 24, 2009).

4. Katherine Albrecht and Liz McIntyre, *Spychips: How Major Corporations and Government Plan to Track Your Every Purchase and Watch Your Every Move* (New York: Penguin, 2006), 7. See also Greg Dixon of ScanSource, quoted in Mark Riehl, "Partners Needed for RFID Success, Says ScanSource," *eChannelLine Daily News,* August 9, 2004, www.echannelline.com (accessed June 11, 2005).

5. Steven Van Fleet, program director of e-packaging and silent commerce at International Paper, believes RFID technology is a huge asset to U.S. retailers. He has stated, "We'll put a radio frequency ID tag on everything that moves in the North American supply chain," quoted in Valigra, "Smart Tags."

6. Valigra, "Smart Tags."

7. Valigra, "Smart Tags."

8. Katherine Albrecht, "Supermarket Cards: The Tip of the Retail Surveillance Iceberg," *Denver University Law Review* 79, no. 4 (Summer 2002): 561, www.spychips.com/documents/Albrecht-Denver-Law.pdf (accessed April 23, 2009).

9. John R. Hind, James M. Matthewson II, and Marcia L. Peters, "Method to Address Security and Privacy Issues of the Use of RFID Systems to Track Consumer Products," U.S. Patent 7,000,834, filed February 21, 2001, and issued February 26, 2006, http://patft.uspto.gov/netacgi/nph-Parser?Sect1=PTO2&Sect2=HITOFF&p=1&u=%2Fnetahtml%2FPTO%2Fsearch-bool.html&r=40&f=G&l=50&co1=AND&d=PTXT&s1=hind.INNM.&OS=IN/hind&RS=IN/hind (accessed April 23, 2009).

10. Vicki Ward, "Coming Everywhere Near You: RFID," http://www-03.ibm.com/industries/financialservices/us/detail/landing/W718379A74748B36.html (accessed March 24, 2009).

11. Valigra, "Smart Tags."

12. Albrecht, "Supermarket Cards," 561.

13. Business Wire, "G&D America's Multi-Application Smart Card Selected for Combined Payroll and 'Virtual Banking,'" All Business, April 24, 1998, www.allbusiness.com/banking-finance/banking-lending-credit-services-cash/6834938-1.html (accessed May 5, 2009).

14. Junko Yoshida, "Euro Bank Notes to Embed RFID Chips by 2005," *EE Times,* December 19, 2001, www.eetimes.com/story/OEG20011219S0016 (accessed March 24, 2009).

15. Rick Karlin, "Chipping Away at Border Wait," *Times Union* (Albany, New York), September 13, 2008, www.timesunion.com/AspStories/story.asp?storyID=720247&category=YTALBANY&BCCode=LOCAL&newsdate=9/14/2008 (accessed April 23, 2009).

16. *Illegal Immigration Reform and Immigrant Responsibility Act of 1996,* Public Law 104–208, Section 656.b.1.A.ii, http://frwebgate.access.gpo.gov/cgi-bin/getdoc.cgi?dbname=104_cong_public_laws&docid=f:publ208.104.pdf, 718 (accessed April 23, 2009).

17. Rebecca Camber, "Barclaycard Unveils Plans for Paying Using Your Mobile Phone, Key Fob, or Fingerprints," *Daily Mail* (London), September 9, 2008, www.daily mail.co.uk/news/article-1053537/Barclaycard-unveils-plans-paying-using-mobile-phone-key-fob-fingerprints.html (accessed April 23, 2009).

18. Albrecht and McIntyre, *Spychips,* 139.

19. Tom Corelis, "U.S. State Department Approves RFID Passports Amidst Privacy Concerns," Daily Tech, January 4, 2008, www.dailytech.com/US+State+Department +Approves+RFID+Passports+Amidst+Privacy+Concerns/article10200.htm (accessed March 24, 2009).

20. Declan McCullagh, "New RFID Travel Cards Could Pose Privacy Threat," ZDNet.com, April 19, 2006, http://news.zdnet.com/2100-9595_22-147694.html (accessed March 27, 2009).

21. Albrecht and McIntyre, *Spychips,* 246.

22. C. P. Snow, "Technology," *New York Times,* March 15, 1971, 37.

23. "Barcelona Clubbers Get Chipped," BBC News, September 29, 2004, http://news .bbc.co.uk/2/hi/technology/3697940.stm (accessed March 30, 2009).

Chapter 4

1. "Wireless Call Location Services—TechNote," November 2007, http://saver.fema.gov/ actions/document.act.aspx?type=file&source=view&actionCode=submit&id=4725 (accessed March 29, 2009).

2. "A 2003 survey of the National Cyber Security Alliance, a Washington-based public interest organization, found that 91 percent of the 120 survey participants had spyware installed on their computers." Rachel Ross, "Hacker Attacked School Computer; Nipissing University Records Accessed by 'Keystroke Logger' Discovered on Server Nipissing Computer Attacked," *Toronto Star,* October 23, 2004.

3. This specialized mouse is manufactured by the California company SecuGen Corporation.

4. Kaitlin Dirrig, "New Airport Agents Check for Danger in Fliers' Facial Expressions," McClatchy Newspapers, August 14, 2007, www.mcclatchydc.com/homepage/story/ 18923.html (accessed March 30, 2009).

5. Dirrig, "New Airport Agents Check for Danger in Fliers' Facial Expressions."

6. Federal Bureau of Investigation, "CODIS—NDIS Statistics," www.fbi.gov/hq/lab/codis/clickmap.htm (accessed March 29, 2009).

7. Howard Safir and Peter Reinharz, "DNA Testing: The Next Big Crime-Busting Breakthrough," *City Journal* (New York City), Winter 2000, www.city-journal.org/html/10_1_dna_testing.html (accessed March 28, 2009).

8. Vince Beiser, "Cops Covet DNA Chip," *Wired,* June 1, 1999, www.wired.com/science/discoveries/news/1999/06/19878 (accessed March 24, 2009).

Chapter 5

1. Patrick S. Poole, "Echelon: America's Secret Global Surveillance Network," Free Republic, December 19, 2005, www.freerepublic.com/focus/f-news/1543354/posts (accessed March 25, 2009).

2. See Nicky Hager, "Exposing the Global Surveillance System," MediaFilter.org, http://mediafilter.org/caq/CAQ59GlobalSnoop.html (accessed March 20, 2009).

3. Echelon involves the United States' NSA, the United Kingdom's General Communications Headquarters (GCHQ), Canada's Communications Security Establishment (CSE), Australia's Defence Signals Directorate (DSD), and New Zealand's General Communications Security Bureau (GCSB).

4. Mike Frost and Michael Gratton, *Spyworld* (Toronto: Doubleday Canada, 1994), 40, 229–34.

5. Hager, "Exposing the Global Surveillance System."

6. Poole, "Echelon."

7. Javier Bernal, "Big Brother Is On-Line: Public and Private Security in the Internet," *Cybersociology Magazine,* August 6, 1999, 1, www.cybersociology.com/files/6_public andprivatesecurity.html (accessed March 20, 2009).

8. Bernal, "Big Brother Is On-Line," 3.

9. Michael Owens, "Echelon Code Word List," Internet Office News, www.internet officenews.com (accessed December 12, 2008); site no longer active.

10. Droidkevin5 (screen name), "Surviving an FBI Lock-In Trace," Everything2, August 4, 2002, http://everything2.com/title/Surviving%2520an%2520FBI%2520Lock-In%2520Trace (accessed March 25, 2009).

11. Kathryn Balint, "Spy in the Sky? That Could Be Echelon," *San Diego Union-Tribune,* October 17, 1999, www.fas.org/sgp/news/1999/10/sdut101799.html (accessed April 24, 2009).

12. Stuart Millar, Richard Norton-Taylor, and Ian Black, "Worldwide Spying Network Is Revealed," *Guardian* (London), May 26, 2001, http://lists.jammed.com/ISN/2001/05/0096.html (accessed June 3, 2009).

13. Andrew Bomford, "Echelon Spy Network Revealed," BBC Radio, November 3, 1999, http://news.bbc.co.uk/1/hi/world/503224.stm (accessed April 24, 2009).

14. Hager, "Exposing the Global Surveillance System."

15. Frost and Gratton, *Spyworld,* 19–20.

16. Christopher Simpson, quoted in Balint, "Spy in the Sky?"

17. Balint, "Spy in the Sky?"

18. *Olmstead et al. v. United States,* 277 U.S. 438 (June 4, 1928), http://supreme.justia.com/us/277/438/case.html (accessed April 24, 2009).

19. *Olmstead et al. v. United States.*

Chapter 6

1. "Real Life Catches Up with *Star Trek,*" HSV Technologies Inc., www.hsvti.com (accessed March 25, 2009).

2. Timothy L. Thomas, "The Mind Has No Firewall," *Parameters: U.S. Army War College Quarterly* 28, no. 1 (Spring 1998): 91–92, www.carlisle.army.mil/USAWC/Parameters/98spring/thomas.htm (accessed April 24, 2009).

3. Richard W. Ziolkowski, "Electromagnetic or Other Directed Energy Pulse Launcher," U.S. Patent 4,959,559, filed March 31, 1989, and issued September 25, 1990, http://patft.uspto.gov/netacgi/nph-Parser?Sect1=PTO2&Sect2=HITOFF&p=1&u=%2Fnetahtml%2FPTO%2Fsearch-bool.html&r=1&f=G&l=50&co1=AND&d=PTXT&s1=4,959,559.PN.&OS=PN/4,959,559&RS=PN/4,959,559 (accessed April 24, 2009).

4. Sharon Weinberger, "The Voice of God Weapon Returns," *Wired,* December 21, 2007, http://blog.wired.com/defense/2007/12/the-voice-of-go.html (accessed March 25, 2009).

5. Patrick Dillon and Majid al-Ghazali, quoted in Bill Dash, "Horrifying U.S. Secret Weapon Unleashed in Baghdad," Rense.com, August 25, 2003, www.rense.com/general40/secret.htm (accessed November 20, 2008).

6. Scott Gourley, "Metal Storm Weapons," *Popular Mechanics,* September 2001, www.popularmechanics.com/technology/military_law/1281426.html (accessed April 24, 2009), with video demonstrations at http://awwar.com/Military-Weapons/Munitions/Metal-Storm-Electronic-Gun-Up-to-10000-Rounds-a-Second (accessed March 30, 2009).

7. "Metal Storm—U.S. Army's 1 Million-Round Gun," www.liveleak.com/view?i=c81c039bcc (accessed March 28, 2009).

8. Noah Shachtman, "When a Gun Is More Than a Gun," *Wired,* March 20, 2003, www.wired.com/politics/law/news/2003/03/58094 (accessed January 15, 2009).

9. Shachtman, "When a Gun Is More Than a Gun."

10. Joseph Farah, "New al-Qaida Threat: Thermobaric Bombs," WorldNetDaily.com, September 29, 2008, www.worldnetdaily.com/index.php?fa=PAGE.view&pageId=76544 (accessed March 27, 2009).

11. Michael Hanlon, "Run Away the Ray-Gun Is Coming: We Test US Army's New Secret Weapon," Mail Online, September 18, 2007, www.dailymail.co.uk/sciencetech/article-482560/Run-away-ray-gun-coming—We-test-US-armys-new-secret-weapon.html (accessed March 29, 2009).

12. Mustavaris (screen name), "Active denial system goes public," Strategy Page, January 25, 2007, www.strategypage.com/militaryforums/29-5320.aspx (accessed March 29, 2009).

13. Ben Ames, "Air Force tunes nonlethal directed-energy weapons," *Military & Aerospace Electronics,* July 2005, 1, http://mae.pennnet.com/articles/article_display.cfm?article_id=231684 (accessed March 29, 2009).

14. See "Valone, Harnessing the Wheelwork of Nature—Tesla's Science of Energy" (2002), www.scribd.com/doc/11539706/Valone-Harnessing-the-Wheelwork-of-Nature-Teslas-Science-of-Energy-2002 (accessed March 30, 2009).

15. Winn Schwartau, *Information Warfare: Cyberterrorism: Protecting Your Personal Security in the Electronic Age* (New York: Thunder's Mouth, 1996), 183–88.

16. The full text of the Convention on the Prohibition of Military or Any Other Hostile Use of Environmental Modification Techniques is available at www.un.org/Docs/asp/ws.asp?m=A/RES/31/72 (accessed March 25, 2009). Click on the language of your choice.

17. Jerry E. Smith, "HAARP Build-Out to 3.6 Million Watt Capacity Complete," April 26, 2006, Rense.com, www.rense.com/general70/haarp.htm (accessed March 30, 2009).

18. The U.S. Air Force has stated that a HAARP transmitter in Alaska will ultimately produce approximately 3.6 million watts of radio frequency power. However, an October 1991 report by the U.S. Air Force Phillips Laboratory, titled "Technical Memorandum 195," described future HAARP tests that could use a staggering power output of up to one hundred billion watts. By way of comparison, a typical radio station commonly broadcasts in the power range of fifty thousand watts. See Amy Worthington, "Chemtrails: Aerosol and Electromagnetic Weapons in the Age of Nuclear War," Centre for Research on Globalization, http://globalresearch.ca/articles/WOR406A.html (accessed April 24, 2009).

19. Frank E. Lowther, "Nuclear-Sized Explosions Without Radiation," U.S. Patent 4,873,928, filed on June 15, 1987, and issued October 17, 1989, http://patft.uspto .gov/netacgi/nph-Parser?Sect1=PTO2&Sect2=HITOFF&p=1&u=%2Fnetahtm l%2FPTO%2Fsearch-bool.html&r=1&f=G&l=50&co1=AND&d=PTXT&s1=4,873, 928.PN.&OS=PN/4,873,928&RS=PN/4,873,928 (accessed April 24, 2009).

20. "Project HAARP: Dangerous Use of Tesla Technology," www.geocities.com/Area 51/Shadowlands/9654/tesla/projecthaarp.html (accessed March 31, 2009).

21. See Robert Ludlum, *The Moscow Vector* (New York: St. Martins Griffin, 2005).

22. "Genetic Warfare, the DNA Bomb and Deadly RNA Interference—The Advanced Warfare," *India Daily,* August 11, 2005, www.indiadaily.com/editorial/4065.asp (accessed April 2, 2009).

23. Hsien-Hsien Lei, "Beware of Genetic Bioviolence," Eye on DNA, www.eyeondna .com/2007/07/09/beware-of-genetic-bioviolence (accessed March 26, 2009).

24. Jose Fermoso, "President Obama Wears Bullet-Resistant Suit at Inaugural," *Wired,* January 21, 2009, http://blog.wired.com/gadgets/2009/01/president-oba-1.html (accessed March 25, 2009).

25. Benjamin Sutherland, "Where's the Sniper?" *Newsweek,* January 26, 2009, www
.newsweek.com/id/180070 (accessed March 30, 2009).

26. Mark Harris, "Networked Helmets Offer Sniper Protection," Techradar.com, March
25, 2009, www.techradar.com/news/portable-devices/networked-helmets-protect-
soldiers-from-snipers-587870 (accessed April 2, 2009).

27. Andy Oppenheimer, "Mini-Nukes: Boom or Bust?" *Bulletin of the Atomic Scientists* 60,
no. 5 (September–October 2004), http://thebulletin.metapress.com/content/125h528
57735n3ju (accessed March 30, 2009).

Chapter 7

1. Adrienne Wilmoth Lerner, "Continuity of Government, United States," Espionage
Information, www.espionageinfo.com/Co-Cop/Continuity-of-Government-United-
States.html (accessed April 3, 2009).

2. "Mount Weather High Point Special Facility (SF)—Mount Weather Emergency
Assistance Center [MWEAC], Western Virginia Office of Controlled Conflict Operations," GlobalSecurity.org, www.globalsecurity.org/wmd/facility/mt_weather.htm
(accessed March 31, 2009).

3. Seymour M. Hersh, "The Iran Plans," *New Yorker,* April 17, 2006, www.new
yorker.com/archive/2006/04/17/060417fa_fact?currentPage=2 (accessed April 3,
2009).

4. Brian Montopoli, "Gates to Be Designated Successor on Inauguration Day," CBS
News Political Hotsheet, January 19, 2009, www.cbsnews.com/blogs/2009/01/19/
politics/politicalhotsheet/entry4734750.shtml (accessed April 25, 2009).

5. James Paul Warburg, www.nowandfutures.com/download/NewWorldOrderQuotes
(accessed March 8, 2009).

6. James P. Warburg, "New World Order Quotes," No World System News Archive,
http://nwsarchive.wordpress.com/2007/09/30/new-world-order-quotes (accessed April
25, 2009).

7. Pierre Teilhard de Chardin, quoted in Louis Pauwels and Jacques Bergier, *Morning of
the Magicians* (New York: Stein and Day, 1964), 55.

8. See "Our Good Conference Guide: Magic Mountains for the Mind," *Economist,*
December 26, 1987, www.bilderberg.org/wdm.htm (accessed April 4, 2009).

9. Richard N. Cooper, Karl Kaiser, and Masataka Kosaka, *Towards a Renovated International System* (New York: Trilateral Task Force, 1977), 193.

10. "Government 101: A Crash Course, Part 7," http://74.125.95.132/search?q= cache:SiVpDq4R4ZkJ:whyamiademocrat.com/PDF/PDFCC7.pdf+President+Bush +warned,+%E2%80%9CFrom+chaos+will+emerge+the+New+World+Order&cd= 1&hl=en&ct=clnk&gl=ca&client=firefox-a (accessed March 30, 2009).

11. Arnold Toynbee, *Surviving the Future* (New York: Oxford University Press, 1971).

12. Zbigniew Brzezinski, *Between Two Ages: America's Role in the Technetronic Era* (New York: Viking, 1970), 72.

13. Brzezinski, *Between Two Ages,* 296.

14. Laurence H. Shoup and William Minter, *Imperial Brain Trust: The Council on Foreign Relations and United States Foreign Policy* (New York: Monthly Review Press, 1977), 112–13.

15. Daniel Brandt, "Clinton, Quigley, and Conspiracy: What's Going On Here?" NameBase NewsLine, no. 1, April–June 1993, www.namebase.org/news01.html (accessed March 30, 2009). For instance, the late David Rockefeller, former head of Chase Manhattan Bank, was chairman of the Council on Foreign Relations and also chairman of the North American division of the Trilateral Commission. See Stephen Gill, *American Hegemony and the Trilateral Commission* (Cambridge: Cambridge University Press, 1990), 236.

16. The *Manchester Union Leader* ran an editorial during the 1979 presidential primaries that warned about the Trilateral Commission: "It is quite clear that this group of extremely powerful men is out to control the world." (See "Government 101: A Crash Course, Part 6," http://whyamiademocrat.com/text/TCC6.html (accessed March 27, 2009).

17. Patrick Wood, "The Trilateral Commission: Usurping Sovereignty," August Review, www.augustreview.com/issues/globalization/the_trilateral_commission:_usurping _sovereignty_2007080373/ (accessed April 25, 2009).

18. Cooper, Kaiser, and Kosaka, *Towards a Renovated International System,* summary available at www.trilateral.org/ProjWork/tfrsums/tfr14.htm (accessed April 25, 2009).

19. Brad Roberts, "The Enigmatic Trilateral Commission: Boon or Bane?" *Millennium— Journal of International Studies* 11 (September 1982): 185–202, http://mil.sagepub .com/cgi/reprint/11/3/185.

20. See "The Facts on the Trilateral Commission Show New World Order Plot," November 3, 2007, Canada Free Press, www.canadafreepress.com/index.php/article/481 (accessed March 29, 2009).

21. The late Henry Morgenthau, a member of the Council on Foreign Relations and a former U.S. treasury secretary, declared, "We can hardly expect the nation-state to make itself superfluous, at least not overnight. Rather, what we must aim for is really nothing more than caretakers of a bankrupt international machine which will have to be transformed slowly into a new one." Henry Morgenthau, quoted on Liberty-Tree .ca, http://quotes.liberty-tree.ca/quote/henry_morgenthau_quote_1c65 (accessed March 25, 2009).

22. Erskine Childers and Brian Urquhart, *Renewing the United Nations System* (Uppsala, Sweden: Dag Hammarskjold Foundation, 1994), 86.

23. Childers and Urquhart, *Renewing the United Nations System,* 19.

24. Childers and Urquhart, *Renewing the United Nations System,* 155.

25. Childers and Urquhart, *Renewing the United Nations System,* 177.

26. "Global Governance Initiative," World Economic Forum, www.weforum.org/en/ initiatives/glocalgovernance/index.htm (accessed April 5, 2009).

27. Mikhail Gorbachev, "World Community Must Seek Solutions in Bosnia, Other Hot Spots," *New York Times,* May 16, 1993, http://archive.deseretnews.com/archive/ 290585/world-community-must-seek-solutions-in-bosnia-other-hot-spots.html (accessed June 2, 2009).

28. Jennifer K. Elsea, "U.S. Policy Regarding the International Criminal Court," Congressional Research Service, August 29, 2006, www.fas.org/sgp/crs/misc/RL31495.pdf (accessed April 25, 2009).

29. Anup Shah, "United States and the International Criminal Court," Global Issues, September 25, 2005, www.globalissues.org/article/490/united-states-and-the-icc (accessed March 30, 2009).

Chapter 8

1. Hal Lindsey, "Was Deadly Iranian Ship Bound for Israel?" WorldNetDaily.com, November 7, 2008, www.wnd.com/index.php?pageId=80313 (accessed April 27, 2009).

2. Andrew Donaldson, "Pirates Die Strangely After Taking Iranian Ship," *Times* (Johannesburg, South Africa), September 28, 2008, www.thetimes.co.za/PrintArticle.aspx ?ID=851953 (accessed April 5, 2009).

3. Jim O'Neill, "The Strange Story of the Ship 'Iran Deyanat,'" Canada Free Press, October 30, 2008, www.canadafreepress.com/index.php/article/5920 (accessed March 25, 2009).

4. Vlad Tepes, "Iranian Ship Was Floating Radiological Bomb Meant for Israel," Vlad Tepes Blog, October 20, 2008, http://vladtepesblog.com/?p=2459 (accessed March 28, 2009).

5. Wu Weilin, "Nuclear Explosion Occurred Near Epicenter of the Sichuan Earthquake, Expert Says," *Epoch Times,* July 14, 2008, http://en.epochtimes.com/n2/china/nuclear-explosion-sichaun-earthquake-1182.html (accessed March 25, 2009).

6. Weilin, "Nuclear Explosion Occurred Near Epicenter."

7. Weilin, "Nuclear Explosion Occurred Near Epicenter."

8. Zhang Haishan, "Earthquake Destroyed China's Largest Military Armory, Says Source," *Epoch Times,* July 9, 2008, www.theepochtimes.com/news/8-7-9/73205.html (accessed March 25, 2009).

9. Conclusions drawn by international scientists support the finding that an unprecedented nuclear accident triggered the 8.1 Sichuan earthquake. See PolarLight2000 (screen name), "Evidence Triggering Sichuan Earthquake by Nuclear Accident Found by Rescue Crew," Now Public, June 2, 2008, www.nowpublic.com/environment/evidence-triggering-sichuan-earthquake-nuclear-accident-found-rescue-crew (accessed March 25, 2009).

Chapter 9

1. Flavius Josephus, *Wars of the Jews, Book 1,* trans. William Whiston (Grand Rapids: Kregel, 1960), 436.

2. Philo, *On Rewards and Punishments,* trans. C. D. Young, in *The Works of Philo, De Praemiis et Poenis* (Peabody, MA: Hendrickson, 1993), 673.

3. Sanhedrin 97b, *Talmud* (London: Soncino, 1987).

4. "Europe: A Rival or an Also-Ran," *Time,* July 13, 1970, www.time.com/time/magazine/article/0,9171,909440-1,00.html (accessed March 25, 2009).

5. "A Peaceful Europe—The Beginnings of Cooperation," World Factbook, www
   .theodora.com/wfbcurrent/european_union/european_union_history.html (accessed
   March 26, 2009).

6. Dana Neacsu, "Romania, Bulgaria, the United States and the European Union: The
   Rules of Empowerment at the Outskirts of Europe," *Brooklyn Journal of International
   Law* 30, no. 1 (2004), www.brooklaw.edu/students/journals/bjil/bjil30i_neacsu.pdf
   (accessed March 29, 2009).

7. Martin Holmes, "William Hague's European Policy," The Bruges Group, www
   .brugesgroup.com/mediacentre/index.live?article=107 (accessed March 25, 2009).

8. Christopher Booker, "Europe and Regulation—The New Totalitarianism" (speech
   given to the Institute of Directors, London, February 1995), quoted in Joe de Courcy,
   Globalists vs. the Nation State (Blimpsfield, UK: Intelligence International, 1995), 1–3.

9. Booker, "Europe and Regulation," 1–2.

10. Booker, "Europe and Regulation," 1–3.

11. Constant Brand and Robert Wielaard, "Conservatives Racing Ahead in EU Parliament
    Voting," the Associated Press, http://news.yahoo.com/s/ap/20090607/ap_on_re_eu/
    european_elections (accessed June 7, 2009).

Chapter 10

1. It has been reported that Congress was mostly unaware that FEMA was spending as
   much as 94 percent of its budget on secret underground installations rather than for
   civilian disaster relief. Reports suggest that FEMA spent as much as $1.3 billion build-
   ing secret leadership bunkers throughout the United States in anticipation of a future
   crisis. See Harry V. Martin, "FEMA—The Secret Government," Free America, 1995,
   http://sonic.net/sentinel/gvcon6.html (accessed March 26, 2009).

2. Martin, "FEMA."

3. Martin, "FEMA." The text of the executive orders listed (except 11921, written by
   Gerald Ford) can be found at www.lib.umich.edu/govdocs/jfkeo/exonum.htm.

4. Joe de Courcy, "NATO's Recipe for War," *Intelligence Digest,* April 30, 1999, 1. *Intelligence Digest* has provided accurate intelligence information and insightful analysis of
   critical situations throughout the world since 1938. Its reports are read by more than
   seventy heads of state and numerous chief executives of multinational corporations.

For more than twenty years I have found de Courcy's research to be impeccably accurate, insightful, and often far in advance of the major news media outlets in identifying significant political and military trends.

5. de Courcy, "NATO's Recipe for War," 1–2.

6. de Courcy, "NATO's Recipe for War," 2.

7. NATO, *The Alliance's Strategic Concept* (Washington DC: North Atlantic Council, April 23–24, 1999), www.nato.int/docu/pr/1999/p99-065e.htm.

8. Final Communique North Atlantic Council Summit, Washington DC, April 24, 1999, http://aei.pitt.edu/508/01/chai47e.html#8.

9. "The number of personnel on peacekeeping missions has grown to 113,000 soldiers, police officers and civilians assigned to 18 missions, from 40,000 in 2000.... The peacekeeping budget has ballooned to $8 billion." Neil MacFarquhar, "In Peacekeeping, a Muddling of the Mission," *New York Times,* February 10, 2009, www.nytimes .com/2009/02/11/world/11peacekeeping.html (accessed April 3, 2009).

10. *Jordan Times,* April 10, 1999, 1.

11. Douglas Hurd, quoted in Jon C. Ryter, *Whatever Happened to America?* (Tampa, FL: Hallberg, 2001), 486–91.

12. "Arms Trade Key Statistics," BBC News, September 15, 2005, http://news.bbc.co .uk/1/hi/uk/4238644.stm (accessed April 27, 2009).

Chapter 11

1. Steve Connor, "Professor Has World's First Silicon Chip Implant," Independent News, August 26, 1998, www.independent.co.uk/news/professor-has-worlds-first-silicon-chip-implant-1174101.html (accessed May 4, 2009).

2. Paul A. Gargano et al., "Personal Tracking and Recovery System," U.S. Patent 5,629,678, filed January 10, 1995, and issued May 13, 1997, http://patft.uspto .gov/netacgi/nph-Parser?Sect1=PTO2&Sect2=HITOFF&p=1&u=%2Fnetahtml %2FPTO%2Fsearch-bool.html&r=1&f=G&l=50&co1=AND&d=PTXT&s1 =5,629,678.PN.&OS=PN/5,629,678&RS=PN/5,629,678 (accessed April 27, 2009).

3. "Applied Digital Solutions Acquires Rights to World's First Digital Device— Company Business and Marketing," BNET, December 20, 1999, http://findarticles .com/p/articles/mi_m0WUB/is_1999_Dec_20/ai_58313649/ (accessed June 4, 2009).

4. Marc Rotenberg, quoted in Richard Stenger, "Tiny Human-Borne Monitoring Device Sparks Privacy Fears," CNN, December 20, 1999, www.cnn.com/1999/TECH/ptech/12/20/implant.device/index.html (accessed March 27, 2009).

5. Shawn Cohen, "Iran May Be Pushing Bogus 'Super' Dollars," *J.*, March 22, 1996, www.jweekly.com/article/full/2813/iran-may-be-pushing-bogus-super-dollars (accessed April 4, 2009).

6. Yiannis Androulakis, "RFID Banknotes," Fleur-de-Coin.com, www.fleur-de-coin.com/eurocoins/rfid.asp (accessed March 27, 2009).

7. "Swift in Figures—SWIFTNet FIN Traffic February 2009 YTD," SWIFT, March 27, 2009, www.swift.com/about_swift/company_information/swift_in_figures/swift _in_figures_archive/swift_in_figures_2009/swift_in_figures_swiftnet_fin_traffic_feb _09/SWIFTinfiguresSWIFTNetFINtrafficfeb09.page?lang=en (accessed March 8, 2009).

8. Santhush Fernando, "Derivative Trading: A Boon to Lankan Financial Market," The Nation on Sunday, www.nation.lk/2009/02/08/busi3.htm (accessed March 28, 2009).

9. Donald H. Rowe, "How to Capture Profits in the Great Bust Ahead: 2010–2011–2012," Wall Street Digest, www.wallstreetdigest.com/investors/index.php (accessed March 28, 2009).

10. John Maynard Keynes, *The Economic Consequences of the Peace* (Charleston, SC: BiblioBazaar, 2007), 103–4.

11. Robert Mundell, "A Decade Later: Asia New Responsibilities in the International Monetary System," speech given in Seoul, South Korea, May 2–3, 2007, quoted in Carl Teichrib, "The Joseph Principle and Crisis Economics," *Forcing Change* 2, no. 9, October 2008, www.crossroad.to/articles2/forcing-change/08/10-crisis-economics .htm.

12. Andrei Zolotov, "For Many Russian Christians Bar Codes Signal Coming of the Antichrist," April 1, 2000, www.christianitytoday.com/ct/2000/aprilweb-only/55.0a .html?start=1 (accessed April 27, 2009).

Chapter 12

1. Michael Kidron and Dan Smith, *The War Atlas: Armed Conflict, Armed Peace* (London: Pan Books, 1983), 5.

2. Anup Shah, "World Military Spending," Global Issues, March 1, 2009, www.global issues.org/article/75/worldmilitarySpending#WorldMilitarySpending (accessed April 3, 2009).

3. Paul (screen name), "Military Spending vs. Foreign Aid: A Post About Priorities," Make Wealth History, May 13, 2008, http://makewealthhistory.org/2008/05/13/ military-spending-vs-foreign-aid-a-post-about-priorities (accessed April 2, 2009). See also Monte (screen name), "The Least, First: What Percent of US Budget Goes to Foreign Aid?" http://masbury.wordpress.com/2008/09/29/what-percent-of-us-budget-goes-to-foreign-aid (accessed March 27, 2009).

4. *Historical Atlas of the Twentieth Century,* http://users.erols.com/mwhite28/20centry .htm (accessed April 4, 2009).

5. Wolfgang K. H. Panofsky, *Two Cultures* (Basel, Switzerland: Birkhäuser, 2006), 189–92.

6. Antony J. Dolman, ed., *Reshaping International Order* (New York: New American Library, 1976), 295–97.

7. Mohamed Bin Huwaidin, "China in the Middle East: Perspectives from the Arab World," *Arab Insight,* www.arabinsight.org/aiarticles/194.pdf (accessed April 5, 2009).

8. "Israelis 'Blew Apart Syrian Nuclear Cache,'" *Sunday Times* (London), September 16, 2007, www.timesonline.co.uk/tol/news/world/middle_east/article2461421.ece (accessed April 5, 2009).

9. "Israeli Intel Chief: Iran Has Long-Range Missiles," MSNBC, April 27, 2006, www .msnbc.msn.com/id/12512391 (accessed April 6, 2009).

10. "Protocol for the Prohibition of the Use in War of Asphyxiating, Poisonous or Other Gases, and of Bacteriological Methods of Warfare," www.bwpp.org/BWnorm/ 1925GenevaProtocol.html (accessed April 3, 2009).

11. Anthony H. Cordesman, *Military Balance in the Middle East—VI* (Westport, CT: Greenwood Publishing Group, 2004), www.snunit.k12.il/north/pdf/MEBalance.pdf (accessed April 5, 2009).

12. "US to Arm Israel and Arab States in $60bn Deal," *Independent* (London), July 31, 2007, www.independent.co.uk/news/world/americas/us-to-arm-israel-and-arab-states-in-60bn-deal-459647.html (accessed April 3, 2009).

13. "Nuclear Weapons," Federation of American Scientists, www.fas.org/nuke/guide/israel/nuke (accessed April 4, 2009).

14. Kidron and Smith, *The War Atlas,* 41–48. Further, some Bible commentators have suggested that the Bible referred to two hundred million horsemen being involved in the battle of Armageddon. But there are less than sixty-five million horses throughout the entire world. However, John's use of the word *horsemen* in Revelation 9:16 refers to the Four Horsemen of the Apocalypse, not to the number of actual horsemen in the armies of the earth. John was indicating that the total size of the future armies of the "Four Horsemen of the Apocalypse" will include two hundred million soldiers led by "the kings of the east," plus an enormous army of soldiers of the Western nations loyal to the Antichrist. See "Number of Horses in the World," *New York Times,* May 5, 1877, http://query.nytimes.com/gst/abstract.html?res=9A0CEEDC123FE63 BBC4D53DFB366838C669FDE (accessed April 4, 2009).

15. Sophia Woodman and Stephanie Ho, "Trafficking of Women in China," Voice of America, September 27, 1995; Dorinda Elliott, "Trying to Stand on Two Feet," *Newsweek,* June 29, 1998; China and Hong Kong—Facts on Trafficking and Prostitution, in Donna M. Hughes et al., *The Factbook on Global Sexual Exploitation* (Brussels: Coalition Against Trafficking in Women, 1999), www.uri.edu/artsci/wms/hughes/china.htm (accessed April 4, 2009).

16. Lesley Stahl, "China: Too Many Men," CBS News, April 16, 2006, www.cbs news.com/stories/2006/04/13/60minutes/main1496589_page3.shtml (accessed April 8, 2009).

Chapter 13

1. George A. Keyworth, quoted in Winn Schwartau, *Information Warfare: Cyberterrorism: Protecting Your Personal Security in the Electronic Age* (New York: Thunder's Mouth, 1996), 103.

2. George W. Landau, Julio Feo, and Akio Hosono, *Latin America at a Crossroads: The Challenge to the Trilateral Countries,* The Triangle Papers, no. 39 (New York: Trilateral Commission, 1990), 12, http://74.125.95.132/search?q=cache:DCi107gOaecJ:www.trilateral.org/library/stacks2/Latin_America_crossroads.pdf.

3. Henry Kissinger, quoted in Charlie Giuliani, "New World Disorder," www.scribd
    .com/doc/7392866/Charlie-Giuliani-New-World-Disorder (accessed April 3, 2009).

4. Thomas R. Eddlem, "GATT's World Trade Oppression," *New American,* September 5,
    1994, http://content.koaa.com/community/listens/post.asp?method=ReplyQuote
    &REPLY_ID=21844&TOPIC_ID=2470&FORUM_ID=5 (accessed March 30,
    2009).

5. Phyllis Schlafly, The Phyllis Schlafly Report, June 1994.

6. George H. W. Bush, "Remarks Announcing the Enterprise for the Americas Initia-
    tive," The American Presidency Project, June 27, 1990, www.presidency.ucsb.edu/
    ws/index.php?pid=18644 (accessed March 30, 2009).

Conclusion

1. Isaac Newton, *Observations upon the Prophecies of Daniel, and the Apocalypse of St. John*
    (London: J. Darby and T. Brown, 1733), 9.

SELECT BIBLIOGRAPHY

Adams, James. *The Next World War: Computers Are the Weapons and the Front Line Is Every-where.* New York: Simon and Schuster, 1998.

———. *Secret Armies: The Full Story of the S. A. S., Delta Force, and Spetznaz.* London: Pan Books, 1988.

Albrecht, Katherine, and Liz McIntyre. *Spychips: How Major Corporations and Government Plan to Track Your Every Move.* New York: Penguin, 2006.

Algosaibi, Ghazi A. *The Gulf Crisis: An Attempt to Understand.* London: Kegan Paul Interna-tional, 1993.

Anderson, Robert. *The Coming Prince.* London: Hodder and Stoughton, 1894.

Arendt, Hannah. *The Origins of Totalitarianism.* Cleveland, OH: World Publishing, 1969.

Armerding, Carl Edwin, and W. Ward Gasque. *Dreams, Visions, and Oracles: The Layman's Guide to Biblical Prophecy.* Grand Rapids: Baker Book House, 1977.

Attali, Jacques. *Millennium: Winners and Losers in the Coming Order.* Translated by Leila Conners and Nathan Gardels. New York: Times Books, 1990.

Auerbach, Leo. *The Babylonian Talmud in Translation.* New York: Philosophical Library, 1944.

Bamford, James. *The Puzzle Palace: Inside the National Security Agency, America's Most Secret Intelligence Organization.* Harmondsworth, Middlesex, UK: Penguin, 1987.

Barnes, Albert. *Notes, Critical, Illustrative, and Practical, on the Book of Daniel.* New York: Leavitt and Allen, 1855.

Baylee, Joseph. *The Times of the Gentiles.* London: James Nisbet, 1871.

Begich, Nick, and James Roderick. *Earth Rising—The Revolution, Toward a Thousand Years of Peace.* Anchorage: Earthpulse, 2000.

Bernstein, Richard, and Ross H. Munro. *The Coming Conflict with China.* New York: Alfred A. Knopf, 1997.

Besant, Walter, and E. H. Palmer. *Jerusalem: The City of Herod and Saladin.* London: Chatto and Windus, 1908.

Blackstone, William E. *Jesus Is Coming.* London: Fleming H. Revell, 1908.

————. *The Millennium: A Discussion of the Question "Do the Scriptures Teach That There Is to Be a Millennium?"* New York: Revell, 1918.

Boutflower, Charles. *In and Around the Book of Daniel.* Grand Rapids: Kregel, 1977.

Bowen, William M., Jr. *Globalism: America's Demise.* Shreveport, LA: Huntington House, 1984.

Bradley, John. *World War III—Strategies, Tactics, and Weapons.* New York: Crescent, 1982.

Bresler, Fenton. *Interpol.* Toronto: Penguin, 1992.

Brown, Lester R., Christopher Flavin, and Hilary French, eds. *State of the World: 1997—A Worldwatch Institute Report on Progress Towards a Sustainable Society.* New York: W. W. Norton, 1997.

Brown, Rebecca. *Prepare for War.* New Kensington, PA: Whitaker, 1992.

Bullinger, E. W. *The Apocalypse, or, The Day of the Lord.* London: Eyre and Spottiswoode, 1909.

Bultema, Harry. *A Commentary on Daniel.* Grand Rapids: Kregel, 1988.

Burkett, Larry. *The Coming Economic Earthquake.* Chicago: Moody, 1991.

Burstein, Daniel. *Euroquake: Europe's Explosive Economic Challenge Will Change the World.* New York: Simon and Schuster, 1991.

Calder, Nigel, ed. *Unless Peace Comes: A Scientific Forecast of New Weapons.* Victoria, Australia: Penguin, 1968.

Cantelon, Willard. *Money Master of the World.* Plainfield, NJ: Logos International, 1976.

Cetron, Marvin, and Owen Davies. *Crystal Globe: The Haves and Have-Nots of the New World Order.* New York: St. Martin's, 1991.

Childers, Erskine, and Brian Urquhart. *Renewing the United Nations System.* Uppsala, Sweden: Dag Hammarskjold Foundation, 1994.

Cook, Terry L. *The Mark of the New World Order.* Indianapolis: Virtue International, 1996.

Cuddy, Dennis Laurence. *Now Is the Dawning of the New Age New World Order.* Oklahoma City: Hearthstone, 1991.

Culver, Robert Duncan. *Daniel and the Latter Days: A Study in Millennialism.* Chicago: Moody, 1977.

Davidson, John. *Discourses on Prophecy.* London: John Murray, 1825.

Dreifus, Henry, and Thomas J. Monk. *Smart Cards: A Guide to Building and Managing Smart Card Applications.* New York: Wiley, 1998.

Dunnigan, James F. *How to Make War: A Comprehensive Guide to Modern Warfare, All the World's Weapons, Armed Forces and Tactics.* New York: William Morrow, 1982.

Elliott, E. B. *Horae Apocalypticae: Or, A Commentary on the Apocalypse, Critical and Historical.* London: Seeley, Burnside, and Seeley, 1846.

Epperson, A. Ralph. *The New World Order.* Tucson, AZ: Publius, 1990.

Fabun, Don. *The Dynamics of Change.* Englewood Cliffs, NJ: Prentice-Hall, 1967.

Fialka, John J. *War by Other Means: Economic Espionage in America.* New York: W. W. Norton, 1997.

Fruchtenbaum, Arnold G. *The Footsteps of the Messiah: A Study of Prophetic Events.* Tustin, CA: Ariel, 1982.

Garfinkel, Simson. *Database Nation: The Death of Privacy in the 21st Century.* Cambridge: O'Reilly and Associates, 2000.

Gill, Stephen. *American Hegemony and the Trilateral Commission.* Cambridge: Cambridge University Press, 1991.

Goetz, William. *The Economy to Come.* Beaverlodge, Alberta, Canada: Horizon House, 1984.

Gorbachev, Mikhail. Perestroika: *New Thinking for Our Country and the World.* New York: Harper and Row, 1987.

Graham, Billy. *Approaching Hoofbeats: The Four Horsemen of the Apocalypse.* Waco, TX: Word, 1983.

Graham, Daniel. *High Frontier.* New York: Tor Books, 1983.

Guinness, H. Grattan. *The Approaching End of the Age.* 8th ed. London: Hodder and Stoughton, 1882.

Haldeman, I. M. *The Signs of the Times.* New York: Charles C. Cook, 1911.

Hersh, Seymour M. *The Samson Option: Israel's Nuclear Arsenal and American Foreign Policy.* New York: Random House, 1991.

Hindson, Ed. *Approaching Armageddon: The World Prepares for War with God.* Eugene, OR: Harvest House, 1997.

———. *End Times, the Middle East, and the New World Order.* Wheaton, IL: Victor Books, 1991.

Hoy, Claire, and Victor Ostrovsky. *By Way of Deception.* Toronto: Stoddart, 1990.

Hunt, Dave. *Global Peace and the Rise of Antichrist.* Eugene, OR: Harvest House, 1990.

Jensen, Carl. *Censored: The News That Didn't Make the News—and Why.* Chapel Hill, NC: Shelburne, 1993.

Josephus, Flavius. *Wars of the Jews.* Translated by William Whiston. Kingston, Ontario: N. G. Ellis, 1844.

Kah, Gary H. *En Route to Global Occupation.* Lafayette, LA: Huntington House, 1992.

Kahn, Herman. *Thinking About the Unthinkable in the 1980s.* New York: Simon and Schuster, 1984.

Kalafian, Michael. *The Prophecy of the Seventy Weeks of the Book of Daniel: A Critical Review of the Prophecy as Viewed by Three Major Theological Interpretations and the Impact of the Book of Daniel on Christology.* Lanham, MD: University Press of America, 1991.

Keegan, John, and Andrew Wheatcroft. *Zones of Conflict: An Atlas of Future Wars.* New York: Simon and Schuster, 1986.

Kidron, Michael. *The New State of the World.* New York: Simon and Schuster, 1991.

Kidron, Michael, and Ronald Segal. *The New State of the World Atlas.* London: Pan Books, 1987.

Kidron, Michael, and Dan Smith. *The New State of War and Peace: An International Atlas.* London: Grafton Books, 1991.

———. *The War Atlas: Armed Conflict, Armed Peace.* London: Pan Books, 1983.

Kincaid, Cliff. *Global Bondage: The U.N. Plan to Rule the World.* Lafayette, LA: Huntington House, 1995.

King, Alexander, and Bertrand Schneider. *The First Global Revolution: A Report by the Council of the Club of Rome.* New York: Pantheon, 1991.

Kirban, Salem. *Before It Happens.* Huntingdon Valley, PA: Second Coming, 1993.

Kurtzman, Joel. *The Death of Money: How the Electronic Economy Has Destabilized the World's Markets and Created Financial Chaos.* Boston: Little, Brown, 1993.

LaHaye, Tim. *No Fear of the Storm: Why Christians Will Escape the Tribulation.* Sisters, OR: Multnomah, 1992.

Larkin, Clarence. *The Book of Daniel.* Philadelphia: Clarence Larkin Estate, 1929.

LaSor, William Sanford. *The Truth About Armageddon: What the Bible Says About the End Times.* Grand Rapids: Baker Book House, 1982.

Levine, Herbert M. *World Politics Debated: A Reader in Contemporary Issues.* New York: McGraw-Hill, 1992.

Lindsay, Hal. *The Final Battle.* Palos Verdes, CA: Western Front, 1995.

Livingstone, Neil C. *The Cult of Counterterrorism: The "Weird World" of Spooks, Counter-terrorists, Adventurers, and the Not-Quite Professionals.* Lexington, KY: Lexington Books, 1990.

Lockyer, Herbert. *All the Messianic Prophecies of the Bible.* Grand Rapids: Zondervan, 1973.

Lowth, William. *A Commentary upon the Prophet Ezekiel.* London: W. Mears, 1773.

Ludwigson, R. *A Survey of Bible Prophecy.* Grand Rapids: Zondervan, 1951.

Malachi, Martin. *The Keys of This Blood: The Struggle for World Dominion Between Pope John Paul II, Mikhail Gorbachev, and the Capitalist West.* New York: Simon and Schuster, 1990.

de Marenches, Alexandre, and David A. Andelman. *The Fourth World War: Diplomacy and Espionage in the Age of Terrorism.* New York: William Morrow, 1992.

de Marenches, Alexandre, and Christine Ochrent. *The Evil Empire: Third World War Now.* London: Sidgwick and Jackson, 1988.

Marshall, Paul, and Lela Gilbert. *Their Blood Cries Out: The Worldwide Tragedy of Modern Christians Who Are Dying for Their Faith.* Dallas: Word, 1997.

McAlvany, Donald S. *Toward a New World Order: The Countdown to Armageddon.* Oklahoma City: Hearthstone, 1990.

McGinn, Bernard. *Anti-Christ: Two Thousand Years of the Human Fascination with Evil.* New York: Harper, 1994.

———. *Visions of the End: Apocalyptic Traditions in the Middle Ages.* New York: Columbia University Press, 1979.

Miller, Charles W. *Today's Technology in Bible Prophecy.* Lansing, MI: TIP, 1990.

Newton, Thomas. *Dissertations on the Prophecies, Which Have Remarkably Been Fulfilled, and at This Time Are Fulfilling in the World.* 2 vols. London: R and R Gilbert, 1817.

Pacepa, Ion. *Red Horizons: Chronicles of a Communist Spy Chief.* Washington DC: Regnery Gateway, 1987.

Patai, Raphael. *The Messiah Texts.* Detroit, MI: Wayne State University Press, 1988.

Payne, J. Barton. *Encyclopedia of Biblical Prophecy.* Grand Rapids: Baker Book House, 1980.

Peccei, Aurelio. *One Hundred Pages for the Future.* New York: New American Library, 1981.

Pentecost, Dwight. *Things to Come: A Study of Biblical Eschatology.* Grand Rapids: Dunham, 1958.

Peters, George. *The Theocratic Kingdom of Our Lord Jesus: The Christ, as Covenanted in the Old Testament and Presented in the New Testament.* Grand Rapids: Kregel, 1957.

Pink, Arthur W. *The Antichrist.* Grand Rapids: Kregel, 1988.

Pusey, E. B. *Daniel the Prophet.* Plymouth, UK: Devonport Society, 1864.

Rae, Debra. *ABCs of Globalism: A Vigilant Christian's Glossary.* Lafayette, LA: Huntington House, 1999.

Randal, Jonathan C. *Going All the Way: Christian Warlords, Israeli Adventurers, and the War in Lebanon.* New York: Vintage Books, 1984.

Reagan, David. *The Master Plan: Making Sense of the Controversies Surrounding Bible Prophecy Today.* Eugene, OR: Harvest House, 1993.

Ritchie, David. *Space War: The Fascinating and Alarming History of the Military Uses of Outer Space.* New York: New American Library, 1982.

Roberts, Alexander, and James Donaldson, eds. *The Ante-Nicene Fathers.* Grand Rapids: Erdmans, 1986.

Robertson, Pat. *The New World Order.* Dallas: Word, 1991.

Saleem, Musa. *Muslims and the New World Order.* London: ISDS Books, 1993.

Schell, Jonathan. *The Fate of the Earth.* New York: Avon, 1982.

Scherman, Nosson, and Meir Zlotowitz, eds. *Daniel: A New Translation with Commentary Anthologized from Talmudic, Midrashic and Rabbinic Sources.* Translated by Hersh Goldwurm. Brooklyn: Mesorah, 1980.

———, eds. *Ezekiel: Yechezkel: A New Translation with Commentary Anthologized from Talmudic, Midrashic and Rabbinic Sources.* Translated by Hersh Goldwurm. Brooklyn: Mesorah, 1980.

Schneier, Bruce, and David Banisar. *The Electronic Privacy Papers: Documents on the Battle for Privacy in the Age of Surveillance.* New York: Wiley, 1997.

Schwartau, Winn. *Information Warfare: Chaos on the Electronic Superhighway.* New York: Thunder's Mouth, 1994.

Seiss, Joseph. *The Apocalypse: A Series of Special Lectures on the Revelation of Jesus Christ.* Philadelphia: Approved Books, 1865.

Shulsky, Abram N., and Gary J. Schmitt. *Silent Warfare: Understanding the World of Intelligence.* Washington DC: Brassey, 1993.

Sklar, Holly, ed. *Trilateralism: The Trilateral Commission and Elite Planning for World Management.* Montreal: Black Rose Books, 1980.

Smith, Barry R. *Final Notice.* Singapore: Barry Smith Family Evangelism, 1985.

Smith, Russell Jack. *The Unknown CIA: My Three Decades with the Agency.* New York: Berkley Books, 1992.

Smith, Wilbur M. *Israeli/Arab Conflict.* Glendale, CA: Regal Books, 1967.

Sukorov, Viktor. *Inside the Soviet Army.* London: Granada, 1984.

Swenson, Richard A. *Hurtling Toward Oblivion: A Logical Argument for the End of the Age.* Colorado Springs: NavPress, 1999.

Tapscott, Don. *The Digital Economy: Promise and Peril in the Age of Networked Intelligence.* New York: McGraw-Hill, 1996.

Taylor, Gordon R. *The Biological Time-Bomb.* London: Thames Hudson, 1968.

Tinbergen, Jan. *Reshaping the International Order: A Report to the Club of Rome.* Scarborough, Ontario: New American Library of Canada, 1976.

Toffler, Alvin. *Power Shift.* New York: Bantam Books, 1990.

Toffler, Alvin, and Heidi Toffler. *War and Anti-War: Survival at the Dawn of the 21st Century.* Boston: Little, Brown, 1993.

Tregelles, S. P. *Remarks on the Prophetic Visions in the Book of Daniel.* Guilford: Billing and Sons, 1965.

Van Impe, Jack. *2001: On the Edge of Eternity.* Dallas, TX: Word, 1996.

Walvoord, John F. Daniel: *The Key to Prophetic Revelation.* Chicago: Moody, 1989.

———. *The Nations in Prophecy.* Grand Rapids: Zondervan, 1976.

Weber, Timothy P. *Living in the Shadow of the Second Coming: American Premillennialism, 1875–1925.* New York: Oxford University Press, 1979.

Whitaker, Reg. *End of Privacy: How Total Surveillance Is Becoming a Reality.* New York: New Press, 1999.

White, John Wesley. *WW III: Signs of the Impending Battle of Armageddon.* Grand Rapids: Zondervan, 1977.

Wright, Susan, ed. *Preventing a Biological Arms Race.* Cambridge, MA: MIT Press, 1990.